The Writing Mirror:

Analyse your writing for self-discovery

Dr Stephanie Carty

PSYCHOLOGY FOR WRITERS SERIES

ABOUT THE AUTHOR

Dr Stephanie Carty is a writer and consultant clinical psychologist in the UK. Her short fiction has won numerous competitions and is widely published. She runs workshops and clinics on applying psychology to different aspects of writing.

Find her at stephaniecarty.com.

Non-fiction

Inside Fictional Minds: Tips from Psychology for Creating Characters. *Ad Hoc Fiction (2021)*

Fiction

Three Sisters of Stone. *Ellipsis (2018)*

(Winner – Best Novella in the Saboteur Awards, written as Stephanie Hutton)

The Peculiarities of Yearning. *Reflex Press (2022). (Finalist - Eyelands Book Awards)*

Shattered. *Bloodhound Books (2023)*

First published by Qualia Press
Psychology for Writers Series

Cover artwork by Louise Ryder-Hall

ISBN 978-1-7384749-1-2

CONTENTS

PROLOGUE

Will you walk with me, along the hall of mirrors of your writing? Consider your catalogue of work. Here's one mirror that elongates your features: disproportionate and stretched – a *you-that-is-not-you* – yet still recognisable. Look to your characters' extremes. The fire-setter, the lover, the vengeful ghost, the martyr. Is this reflection an exaggerated version of something residing within? Disallowed parts may seek a new home. Are there any elements to pull from the mirror and own?

Next, here's a mirror with an inbuilt filter: a version you long to become or regret having passed. Perhaps a character who achieves resolution or hope in the story's climax. Could this trajectory map out your own desired path? Can your stories give you a lesson when times are hard? You may feel unworthy of this ending, permitting it only in fiction. Walk into the mirror.

Do you see no resemblance in the next? Remember, a mirror is not a likeness but an opposite. In this back-to-front world, your stories may play with the dark twin of your own qualities and experiences to tell you what you are not (which may be the same as what you long for).

Stay still now and stare. Your face contorts. Just as a mirror image is unreliable, the character you write may not represent like for like. We have metaphorical minds. Without our conscious awareness, we pour the sand of ourselves into differently shaped glass.

You are drawn to return to one mirror. Does it diminish, stretch, beautify? Does it offer hope or explore lost chances? Does it reverse to reveal? Perhaps you may wish to wonder why. And once in a while, you could decant your ink into a different mirror, place your hand into its shimmering surface, and shape a new you.[1]

INTRODUCTION

If dreams are the royal road to the unconscious mind as proposed by Freud,[2] then what are the stories that we write? Perhaps winding, bramble-backed paths, which lead from the part of our mind that is secret from us, to the page.

In writing, as in dreams, there is both the manifest content (what the story appears to be about) and the latent content (symbolic meaning). In psychotherapy, there is a focus on both process and content with a client, to tap into an understanding of unconscious drivers of behaviour. Likewise, a focus on the process of *how* we write as well as the content of *what* we write can be revealing of the self. [3]

This book is for writers who are curious about their inner world and how it relates to their writing habits, emotional responses, beliefs about their work and themselves as a writer, and relationship with writing. It provides reflective tasks as a window into aspects of the self.

Part one focuses on process – *how* we write. Consider what lies behind your writing behaviours and responses. We will start with the fantasy of the perfect writing circumstances and end the section considering how perfectionism or avoiding full effort may impact on you.

Part two considers *what* you write. We will explore key themes in your writing and how your work taps into (or avoids) factors such as power and yearnings.

Part three relates to discovery. We will focus on what you can learn about yourself from paying attention to your relationship with writing, the ways it may hold up a mirror to you, and the function writing plays in your life. This section aims to analyse your writer-self to illuminate ways you can gain a deeper understanding of who you are and how you choose to act.

The purpose of reading this workbook is to increase your insight into the writer-self and how some patterns may also resonate with other aspects of your life. It is neither an academic text nor a self-help book but an opportunity to take the time to focus inwards.

There are no right or wrong answers to the tasks set. Take note of your emotional reactions to them as communication from within. Finally, you are invited to treat yourself with observant compassion along the way.

Part 1: Process

How you write

THE PERFECT WRITING CONDITIONS

The idea of the perfect circumstances in which to write can linger at the edges of our sighs and frustration. *If only... When I have... That later time when I can...*

The warning is in the word *perfect* – that aspirational cosh.

Here is the story a writer may tell herself about writing conditions:

I am sound-sensitive so I need quiet: no music, no children, no sniffing library-dwellers. Comfort is vital. Choice and control are my familiar friends. Perhaps some trees in the background to root me into nature and allow the effortless flow to emerge over the course of at least a whole day, where I will be in the right state of mind to be consumed by my work.

In this fantasy, the route to writing is facilitated by a cottage in the woods or at least a separate space, includes physical and emotional comfort, and no interruptions. It has a fairy-tale quality to it in which writing is a mystical experience away from everyday life. Ease of writing is prioritised as a signal that optimal conditions are reached: this is how things 'should be'. The other-worldliness of it is both alluring and – for the vast majority of the time – unachievable.

What if we become scientists of ourselves? Press pause on the kidnapper's demands: no writing shall flow until you pay the sum of six child-free hours, an oak desk in a library that smells of history, the show-home house in order, all pain and fatigue wrapped tightly in medication and denial.

What answer does reality give in reply when you take time to map out the actual moments that have led steadily to words created on a page, or a pruning of thorns in editing?

Impact of beliefs

The stories we tell ourselves about if and when we can write may influence our ability to actually write. A belief that we will be able to do something (in this case, 'creative self-efficacy'[4]) impacts on effort, persistence, efficiency, motivation and managing associated emotions.[5]

To break it down, one version of this fantasy of the perfect conditions includes the beliefs that

- Writing should take place somewhere special while feeling good.

- Solitude and significant periods of time are the best route to ensure flow.
- Comfort and control are essential to productivity.
- 'Real' writing flows effortlessly in the right circumstances.

On closer examination, this writer may uncover the reality:

A significant proportion of this writer's time occurred propped up in bed with a laptop on her knee, exhausted from the day, willing the children to stay asleep. Outside of the home, the most productive circumstances tended to be those where she was trapped: the library with too many bags to drag around nearby shops, a train and, much to her surprise, at a soft play centre. Amid screeches, demands to 'look at me' and tinny music, writing was the lesser evil. On reflection, she realises she can write when tired, grumpy, cheerful or bored. Sometimes the writing flows easily; other times it is slow and effortful. In the final product, she can't distinguish between the two chunks despite the story she often tells herself that 'easy, natural' writing is 'better'. Rather than choice and control, she works more productively with an external deadline or expectation. On a self-made writing retreat with friends in a beautiful location, the sum total of writing in two days of heaven was zero words.

By assessing real-world experiences of writing, some beliefs about a writer's own 'necessary conditions' can be shattered. Holding on too tightly to the fantasy can leave us trapped in procrastination, avoidance and under-performing due to our beliefs.

The fantasy writer-self as a creative hermit (and your own fantasy, whatever that is) may well not match the reality. This knowledge can be liberating and enabling.

The psychological evidence suggests that changing our story about our ability to write under broader circumstances may actually improve performance to match this expectation.[6]

*What are your ideal writing conditions? Once you have a short list, reread it and add any images or details that come to mind.

*What is the cost to you and your work if you hold too tightly to the ideal of ‘perfect writing conditions’?

*Keep a log of or retrospectively list the conditions under which you have managed to write.

Are there some common conditions that you could reproduce?

*Are there any elements that you could challenge or experiment with changing (e.g. *I must have silence, it must be early morning, I must have a notebook and favourite pen, I can't be in public, I have to plan what I'm going to write first*)?

*What have you learned about yourself by checking the evidence? Is your fantasy of ideal writing conditions fairly accurate or does experimentation show that a broader set of conditions can be effective?

RULES FOR WRITING PROCESS

We like rules. There's a solidity to them that instructs our actions. Rules work as a navigation tool: they can do the work of thinking for us and shield us from the messiness of real life.

We don't always know what our own rules are. We soak them up from living in a world where things seem to work a certain way. They remain unnoticed and therefore their role in governing our behaviours remains unquestioned. The *shoulds* and *musts* of rules give them the appearance of universality. *It is just the way things are. Or the way things should be*.[7]

We have our own rules for both how and what we write. Let's focus on the former: we have internalised rules about how, when and why we write, what it should feel like, what must happen next. By this, I don't mean rules such as 'show, don't tell' but rather *'I should enjoy it / plot in advance / feel motivated / only write beautiful sentences / feel like I know what I'm doing.'*

In order to take a personal approach to rules in writing, it is useful to consider the limitations we have created around what counts as writing, who or what it should be for, how it should feel to write or have written, and what ought to happen to our work to validate it. (It can be useful to notice the '*shoulds, oughts, musts*' as a way of telling you that something is a rule.)

In order to decide whether you wish to keep to your own rules – to assess if they are useful to you – the first step is to become aware of them in detail. You can only make choices when you know there is a choice to be made.

We also like to break rules – to hurl our soft selves against the brickwork of them. When does this happen and what is the outcome?

Do you feel like a rule-maker, the king or queen of your own castle? Perhaps not. Perhaps it seems that the government of publishing makes the rules and you bow to its authority. But what if you were to reach inside and edit your rulebook? I invite you to a little anarchy from inside your own castle.

What counts?

What we believe 'counts' as writing will be different for each of us, informed by the pond we've swum in and the beliefs of those who've influenced us (whether we realise that or not). We construct our own definition of what counts, which then impacts on our sense of satisfaction, achievement and therefore our motivation.

For example, does it only count if you have 'something to show for it'? Does that mean new words only? Do editing notes count? Whispers of ideas in half-formed notes on a phone? Voice notes? Reading for research? Daydreaming about plot or characters while folding towels or pretending to listen to a description of Minecraft?

Rules of achievement

Perhaps you are trapped in the sticky web of preferring your writing to 'achieve' something: to create some change or reflection in the reader or to be 'proven' as good by being published or winning a prize. Although not fundamentally bad or a problem, this rule of achievement means that writing is not permitted without also contemplating how it will be seen and used *externally*. On reflection, this 'other' rather than 'self' focus, a practical rather than pleasure focus, a need for legitimacy by causing change externally, is likely to be reflected in other parts of your life. This could indicate the need to work on valuing your own experiences, giving yourself permission to play and gaining satisfaction from yourself rather than from external judgement. We will return to these ideas in later sections of the workbook.

Origin of rules

Rules are created by experiences. Once upon a time, these rules belonged to somebody else. Over time, we absorb them to the point that they become our own: unquestioned and powerful.

Uncovering rules

If you are interested in investigating your rules around the writing process, it can be useful to step back and help those beliefs come into conscious awareness. What thoughts emerge when you think about writing? And what's the very next thought that jumps in? Remember, the rules are created from all the messages we've received directly and indirectly. They can even contradict one another.

Here are some examples:

'Some people say they love to write, but I don't; it can feel like a chore. Oh, no, I'm not as in love with writing as a real writer.'

RULE: A writer should enjoy writing and feel compelled to write.

This belief could be demotivating, increase avoidance or lead to concerns regarding not being a legitimate writer. You can see how this could spiral into behavioural and emotional changes.

'I wish it wasn't the family birthdays next week so I could get some writing done. What a horrible daughter I am, wanting to selfishly spend time on writing rather than with my own elderly parents.'

RULE: Family should come first over writing, which is a luxury or a side hustle.

The labelling of writing as a 'luxury' could reduce the time dedicated to it and increase feelings of frustration in relation to other life demands and the act of writing.

'I'll know it's the right project when I'm consumed by it. This piece isn't grabbing me any more; I think I'll try another idea.'

RULE: Projects should be highly motivating the whole way through: abandon any that don't make you feel this way.

You could fall into the trap of repeatedly starting new writing projects and never feeling 'consumed' enough to complete them, if you believe that this is a signifier of what's worthy of your time.

Here are some examples of beliefs while writing, editing or rereading:

It's arrogant to think that your own writing is good.

This isn't as good as (other writer) / (previous writing).

I should be better than this by now.

If it isn't good enough, it should be abandoned.

I should get an excited feeling, otherwise it's a sign of failure.

I must keep editing until the opening is perfect.

What should happen next?

We can place extreme pressure on ourselves with rigid ideas around timescales, agents, competitions, publishing and so on. Any deviation from what we think 'should' happen can knock some people, while others take it in their stride. So, what can we learn about ourselves through these reactions?

One difference between those who struggle more or less with difficult situations such as rejection is the rigidity with which the rule is held. The rules can be thought of in the format *'I should / must / shouldn't... otherwise...'*.

*'**I should** get an agent within six months of trying, **otherwise** it means this book is no good and I'll bin it.'*

One technique of increasing flexibility is to check how easily you can switch *'should'* to *'I'd like…'* and change *'otherwise'* to *'but if not…'*.

*'**I would like** to get an agent within six months, **but if not** then I'll give it six more months / switch the project I'm working on to energise me / take it back to my beta readers / speak to others in the same boat to see how that compares.'*

In the example given, you can see it's not a case of 'positive thinking' that is helpful. In fact, the book may not be ready or right for market – we don't know. What the second example demonstrates is flexibility of thought and action – that there are multiple possibilities of what to do next.

If you find the task challenging, this indicates it's an area you might want to practise working on.

Reflections in other areas of life

A further step back into non-writing life could be useful now. In what ways may similar rules impact in other areas of life? For example, do you tell yourself that family and work life should always be 'enjoyable' or there's something wrong? Do you minimise certain parts of what you enjoy and prioritise others' needs? Do you give up on hobbies, work or relationships quickly when the exciting early phase ends or you experience any challenge?

It's likely that the rigidity of rules and the distress caused when things don't work out also impacts you in other areas of life. Fortunately, these rules are not set forever and can be adjusted to be more helpful.

The rules are often so embedded in daily life that you do not realise that they are held or what impact they have. Perhaps starting with writing rules and working backwards will reveal aspects of how we run our lives more generally. Then we can decide if that's helpful and healthy or whether we want to loosen our grip on the rigidity of these rules and try something new.

*How much of a priority is writing allowed to be in your life?

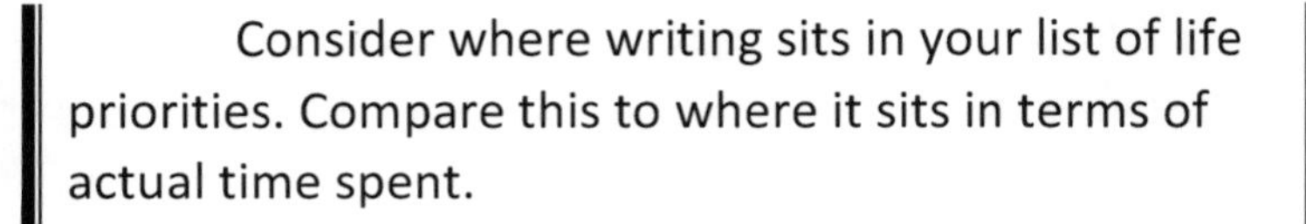
Consider where writing sits in your list of life priorities. Compare this to where it sits in terms of actual time spent.

What rules might impact any difference between value and time spent (outside of practical concerns such as work, health, other commitments)?

I should, shouldn't, must, ought to…

*What are your rules about how you should feel and act while writing?

*What are your rules around how you should feel about your work as you plan, write or edit?

Write these out as *'I should... otherwise...'*

Are any of those unhelpful?

What would it look like to be more flexible? *'I'd like to... but if not...'*

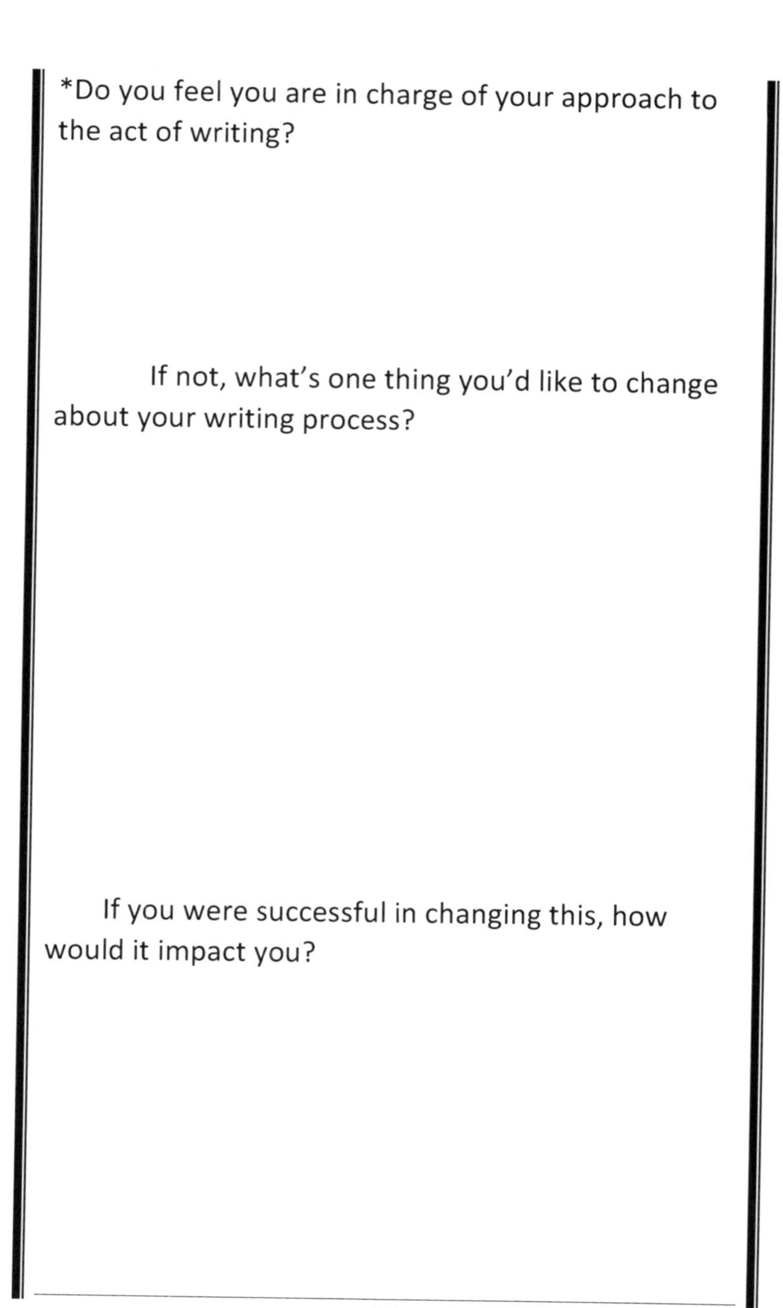

*Do you feel you are in charge of your approach to the act of writing?

If not, what's one thing you'd like to change about your writing process?

If you were successful in changing this, how would it impact you?

*Are there any links between your rules for writing and rules for the rest of your life?

What do your answers tell you to reflect on? How might they help you to loosen your grip upon certain aspects?

THE BLANK PAGE

Is the blank page an invitation to create or an old, white man judging your actions? Does it give you a sense of freedom and fresh start or does it paralyse you? Knowing the nature of your relationship with the blank page can help direct your actions.

At the most fundamental level, consider what your version of a blank page is. Is it the empty screen on your laptop with the flashing cursor? Is it a fresh page in a notebook? Just spending a few minutes pondering what initially seems like a pointless question with a clear answer can lead to new considerations. What about the 'notes' section on your phone, or if you log a dream or conversation? For those who are more visual in their creative imagination, do ideas come with the sense you're filling a blank page with images, or could that be the case simply by deciding it?

We can become scientists of ourselves when we take the time to notice our relationship to words, images, actions and what they mean or say to us. You don't necessarily need to change a single thing about what you perceive or believe or how you act, but the *noticing in itself* puts you into observer mode, whereby you can learn and choose what to do next rather than continue on autopilot.

Anxiety

The concept 'anxiety is the dizziness of freedom'[8] may resonate when you start a writing task, in that the boundless possibilities of the blank page may be experienced as overwhelming.

The beliefs we hold about the blank page (and everything else in our writing life) will impact how anxious we get about it. Now, surely anxiety and stress are bad for creativity? Well, as with most things, the relationship between the two may not be that simple. In many domains of life, there appears to be a curvilinear relationship between level of anxiety and performance, so that performance initially increases with anxiety or stress up to a certain point (think of the focus of a deadline or a piece of work that's very meaningful to you) but then performance starts to dip and then crash if anxiety becomes too high.

There may be times when we label a feeling as 'anxiety' when perhaps what we mean is excitement, being pushed out of our comfort zone, energised, dysregulated or similar.

One of the main tasks of our minds is to keep us safe, and the warning signal of anxiety is vital at times. However, the 'alert' system in the brain can be far more sensitive in some people than in others. For example, those who have had to cope with multiple adverse events, stressors and trauma may be more alert to the possibility of danger at a lower threshold than others, in order to reduce risk.[9] In that case, the bodily system can benefit from being soothed, to signal that you're not in literal danger. Your nervous system needs to be as regulated as possible to allow higher-level functions, such as planning and writing, to work well.

Possibilities

Alternatively, you may be drawn to the blank page and its possibilities. Perhaps it is hard to stay focused on one task as you hear the call of the new. You may find yourself frequently jumping to the next idea, immersed in the early stages, until that too seems to stagnate. This is somewhat like the thrill of the early stages in a romantic relationship, filled with possibility, hope and excitement compared to the solid humdrum of a longer-term relationship with practicalities to contend with. This flitting could also be a form of avoidance of failure, which we will consider later.

Executive functioning

Writers differ in how their brains function. One relevant area of difference can be executive functioning skills. These are a set of cognitive processes, including initiation (starting a task), attention, working (short-term) memory, planning, self-monitoring and self-regulation.[10] Difficulties in executive functioning skills are more likely to be encountered by people with a diagnosis of autism or ADHD or who have had adverse early childhood experiences.[11] The blank page can be more challenging for writers with executive functioning difficulties. These issues can be exacerbated by anxiety, such as that which comes if you put intense pressure on yourself or treat yourself harshly when you struggle with starting a new project.

'Blank pages' outside of writing

You may experience a sense of being frozen or avoiding new starts in other areas of your life. For example, *'there's no point trying this hobby – I'll be no good'* or *'I can't face starting a new relationship as the same thing will probably happen again.'* Notice the presumptions that might be fuelling this avoidance of a new start. The first step to opening up to the freedom of possibilities is to notice how much you restrict them.

*What comes to mind when you imagine the blank page?

Notice the image or description and whether that's a narrow definition.

What is the impact on your body or breathing?

Does it give a sense of possibility and excitement or a sense of being frozen?

*If the blank page causes you to freeze, play with ways designed to help you with the initiation of a task:

e.g. doodling, bullet points with ideas, a quote or picture prompt at the top, a set of instructions to yourself, write 'top secret, not for sharing', copy a line you have written from another piece as the starting point to delete later, list random words that appeal to you to include in the opening, and so on.

*Draw or write out a new way of looking at the front page to help your mind build new associations:

e.g. you could create a spider diagram that includes words such as ‘freedom’, ‘exciting’, ‘permission’. Or make a collage around a picture of a notebook or blinking cursor on your laptop.

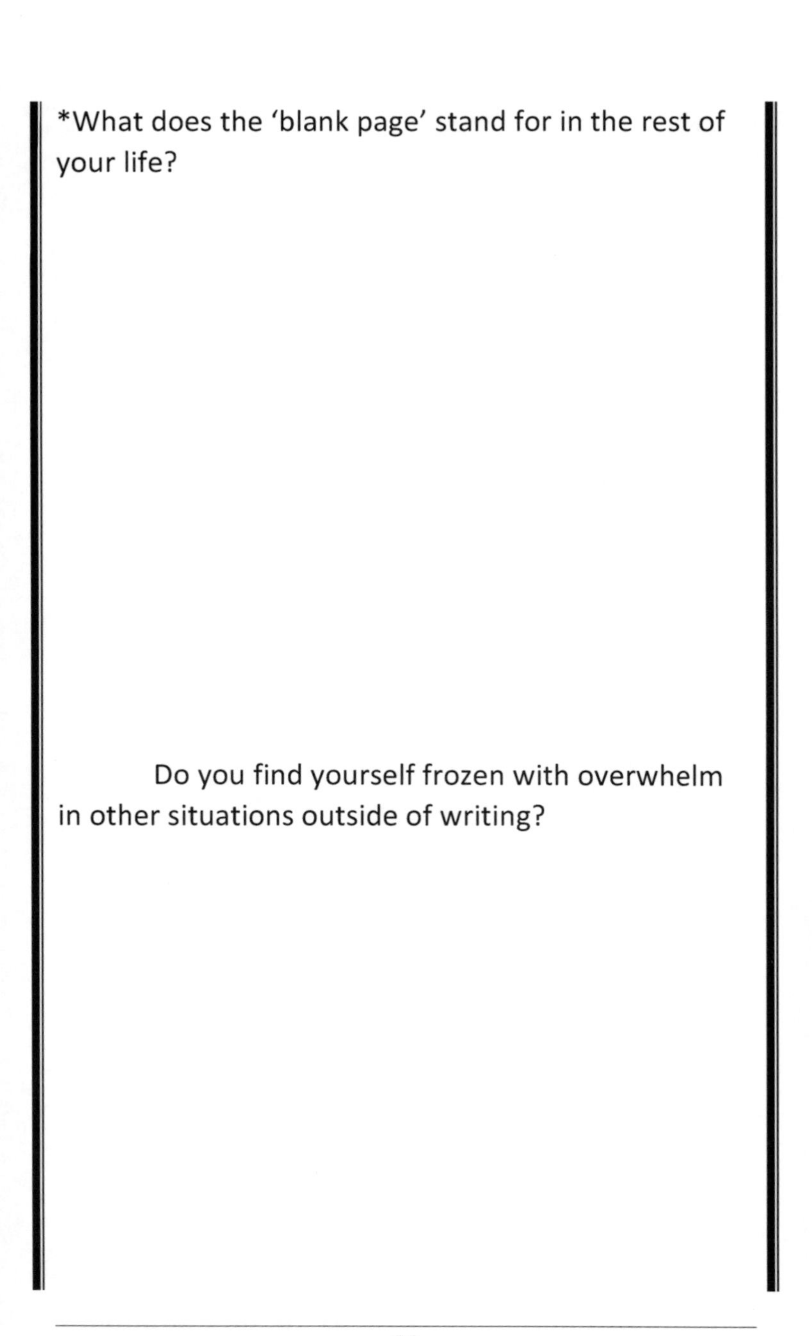

*What does the 'blank page' stand for in the rest of your life?

Do you find yourself frozen with overwhelm in other situations outside of writing?

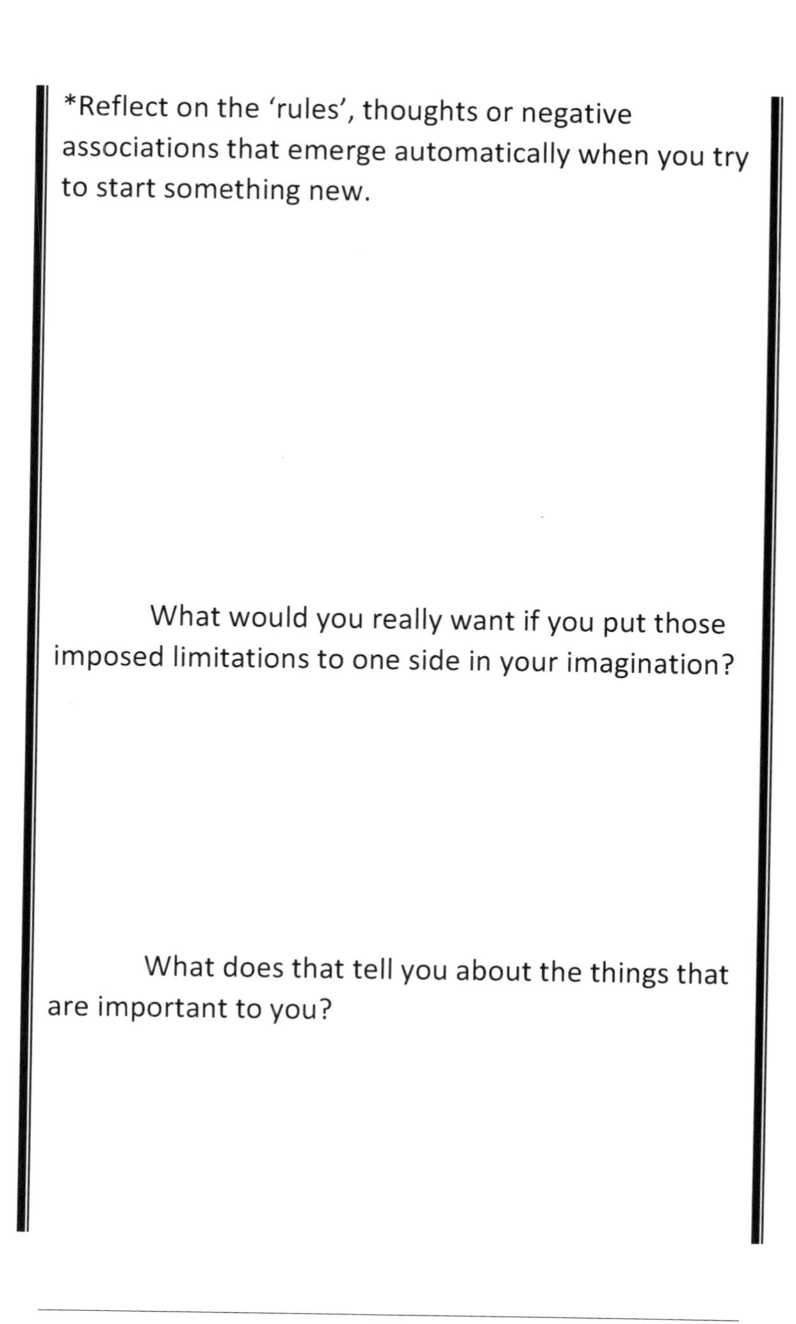

*Reflect on the 'rules', thoughts or negative associations that emerge automatically when you try to start something new.

What would you really want if you put those imposed limitations to one side in your imagination?

What does that tell you about the things that are important to you?

Being swept up by a flow state – as if being carried down a river without exertion, each bend bringing new and unexpected scenery – can be a wonderful experience for a writer.

What emerges during creative flow has been shown to sometimes be a surprise to the writer.[12] This is a state where time can become distorted as writing emerges almost effortlessly and without being hampered by self-consciousness or fear.[13] However, trying to 'force' this state from a place of pressure is unlikely to be effective.

Enhancing opportunities for flow

You can't 'force' yourself to sneeze when you feel like you need to, but for a third of people, looking at a bright light will help the sneeze arrive.[14] So how can you increase the chances of entering a creative flow state if you wish to?

The psychologist Csikszentmihalyi stated that '[f]low occurs in that delicate zone between boredom and anxiety'.[15] He suggested we work best and are more likely to achieve a flow state when demands are slightly higher than usual to avoid apathy, but not so high as to cause anxiety.

Flow is more likely to be elicited in the following conditions:[16]

- Sufficient challenge at a level that matches (perceived) skill.
- Challenges in the task are perceived as 'opportunities for action'.
- A focus away from everyday life with high concentration.
- A clear goal.
- A sense of personal control.
- Rewarding and enjoyable.

Flow is associated with an increased sense of playfulness[17] and is three times more likely to occur during work-related tasks compared to recreational ones.[18] This suggests that the way in which we approach our writing, as well as our beliefs around our capability to meet the challenges and whether or not it counts as 'work', could influence the likelihood of a flow state emerging.

The ebb and flow while writing

Writing flow changes across situations. What if all experiences of writing were equally valid – sometimes pouring out with seemingly little effort and other times the hard slog of trying to walk underwater?

Pay attention to what beliefs emerge about writing that occurs in a flow state (if that's something you experience) or what you believe it means when each word seems to take huge effort. Our brains are wired to try to make sense of experiences but can sometimes draw false conclusions.

Let's say it has been a slow day, with each sentence taking a long time and then being deemed unworthy, hence deleted. In a group of writers who share the same lack of flow, each person might attribute their experience to something different: fatigue, mood, personality, heat, lack of ability, the wrong project, a need for a change of scene, a sign to persevere and break through, a sign to give up for the day and watch Netflix, a failure in the work, a failure in the self, a normal day for a writer mid-project, a chance to reread earlier drafts. And with each of the above come different kinds of potential behaviour: eat, sleep, problem-solve with a friend, read a favourite book, seek reassurance, get outdoors, delete the entire story, settle down to three more hours of focus, and so on.

Beliefs are shaped across a lifetime, influenced by multiple external and internal factors, including mood state, body state, availability of choice and support, and all lead to different lines of action and emotion.

*Have you had the experience of flow in your writing life?

What was the experience like?

What kind of writing emerged?

*Do you hold a belief that writing during 'flow' is what counts, or that it is somehow superior or what 'real writers' experience?

Speak with other writers to find out how much of their work is written while in a more effortful state.

*Review the list of conditions that make flow more likely and see if any could be increased by a change in your approach to writing:

- Sufficient challenge at a level that matches (perceived) skill

- Challenges in the task are perceived as 'opportunities for action'

- A focus away from everyday life with high concentration

- A clear goal

- A sense of personal control

- Rewarding and enjoyable

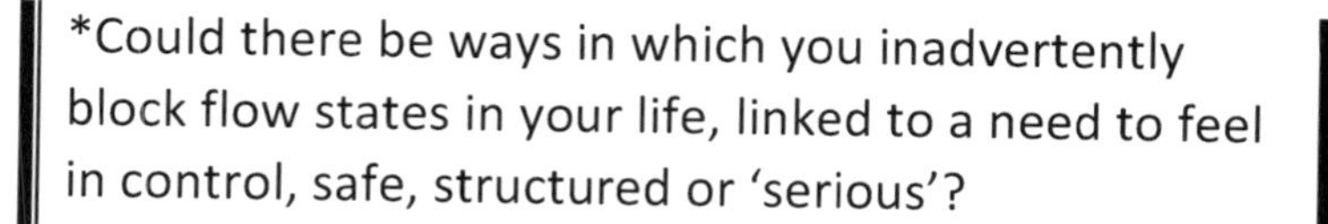
*Could there be ways in which you inadvertently block flow states in your life, linked to a need to feel in control, safe, structured or 'serious'?

What could you do to that would help you feel safe enough to experiment with letting go for a short time, to allow your creative mind the space to wander and take you on a journey?

The Perceiving 'I'

The end goal of writing is often to be read by other people. But do you find that these 'others' are involved far earlier? That it's as if these invisible judges frown at your notebooks, your daydreaming of possible new story ideas, or your first draft? Whose 'eyes' are on you?

Or the sense of judgement may seem as if it's totally self-created – a part of your own mind that becomes an internal critic.

The lens through which we write will impact on how, what and even *if* we write. Some writing projects can leave us feeling more exposed and vulnerable to judgement than others, so these can be the times we are most impacted.

We've already considered the rules that act as scaffolding for our beliefs as to how we *should, ought to, mustn't* write and feel, and the impact of these. Now let's consider judging thoughts or appraisals that may emerge as you write, edit or reread your own work.

Thoughts centred on self

I can't do it.

I hate this project / my writing / this feeling.

I wish I could be working on something else.

This is impossible to finish / make good enough.

I can't figure out where to take this.

Why did I ever bother.

I'll never write as well as (X).

If I stop writing and wait, the answers will come to me eventually.

There's a seed here that I can grow.

It's good enough.

My core message comes through here.

I like the way that sounds when I say it out loud.

I can't wait to continue / polish this.

Thoughts centred on others' reactions

What's the point, when the publishing system is so broken or not for people like me.

This doesn't matter to anybody.

This will disappoint people.

If I'm bored, then the reader will be.

I'm giving away too much of myself.

The reader will think this is about me.

I shouldn't write something so dark / commercial / complicated.

This section will help the reader understand other people.

I think this will make the (reader / editor / agent / publisher) feel (X emotion).

*Which of these thoughts seem familiar to you?

For each one that seems familiar, what's the likely impact on your emotion, behaviour and further thoughts about the writing project or yourself as a writer?

What other common thoughts emerge when you plan, write, reread or edit? It may help to log them as they occur.

You may choose to notice these thoughts, reason with them where they are unhelpful, or simply pull back from them, as if you're flying above, so they can exist without you being pulled into reacting to them. Other thoughts may be encouraging and motivate you. Can you increase your use or focus on these in the future?

The origins of our lens

From a young age, and continuing through our lives, we receive feedback from others. Family members, peers, teachers and strangers all contribute with comments and behaviours that provide information about what is deemed 'unacceptable'. We absorb these messages without intent: a social sponge for judgement.

The family, social and cultural contexts play a significant role in what messages we receive. For example, is a child praised for reading aloud a poem they have written or told not to show off? Are they judged on the content of what they produced for homework or the amount of effort put in? Are errors highlighted in a shaming way or as a learning opportunity? Small interactions happen hundreds of thousands of times to build each person's individual perceptions and beliefs.

For some people, their experiences mean they don't trust their own judgement, or they have learned to rely heavily on the appraisal of others. To some extent, this is what our education system is geared up for!

If you feel a lack of anchor in trusting your own perspective, you may find that you are constantly seeking the opinion of others (either in real life or in your imagination). Most writers do seek out support and opinion from others. But perhaps you find that your focus is always on the external, that you can be crushed by one negative comment, or frozen at the thought of a frown, review or rejection, so that it's hard to trust your own judgement at all.

*As you are writing, editing or reading back over your work, where does the judgement of it seem to come from?

Who are you imagining responding?

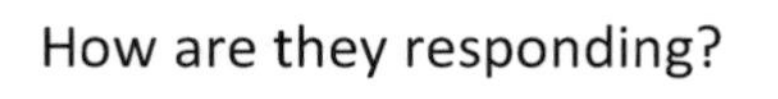

How are they responding?

If it seems it's your own mind, what do you notice about the tone of voice in your head? Does this remind you of a particular person or role – real or imagined? (e.g. strict teacher)

*What is the impact of these judgements of your work on what you think, how you feel and what you do next?

*Do these same internal or imagined criticisms arise in other areas of your life?

*In what ways have you (or could you) play with changing the tone or content of the internal or imagined judgemental voice?

*What happens if you let the internal comments and criticisms flow past without being pulled into them, as if scrolling on social media without engaging with a negative post?

*Do you (or could you) introduce a more compassionate voice when you evaluate your work (in the manner you'd speak to a loved one)?

It may be that you are unused to focusing on what you are proud of, value or enjoy, as your default (learned) position has been to prioritise other people's opinion.

When you review your work, you may have a brain that has learned to be in 'threat mode' – hyper-focused on seeking out and responding to possible danger.[19] This impacts negatively on self-appraisal as well as leading you to guess how others will react. A soothed, regulated nervous system is the best place to put yourself in to form a thoughtful, balanced opinion of your work.

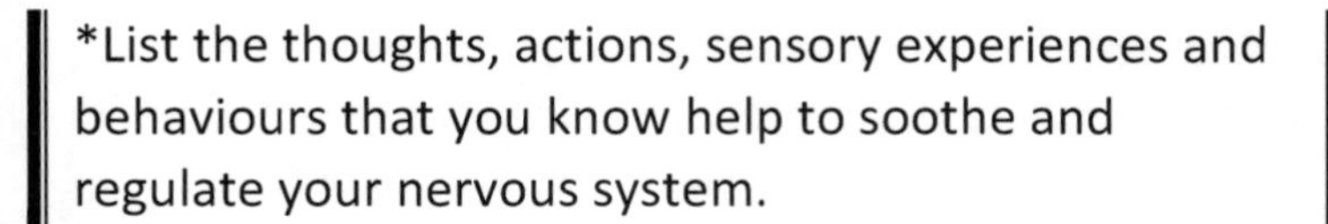

*List the thoughts, actions, sensory experiences and behaviours that you know help to soothe and regulate your nervous system.

When you use one of your helpful soothers, what do you notice happens to the judgemental voice related to writing?

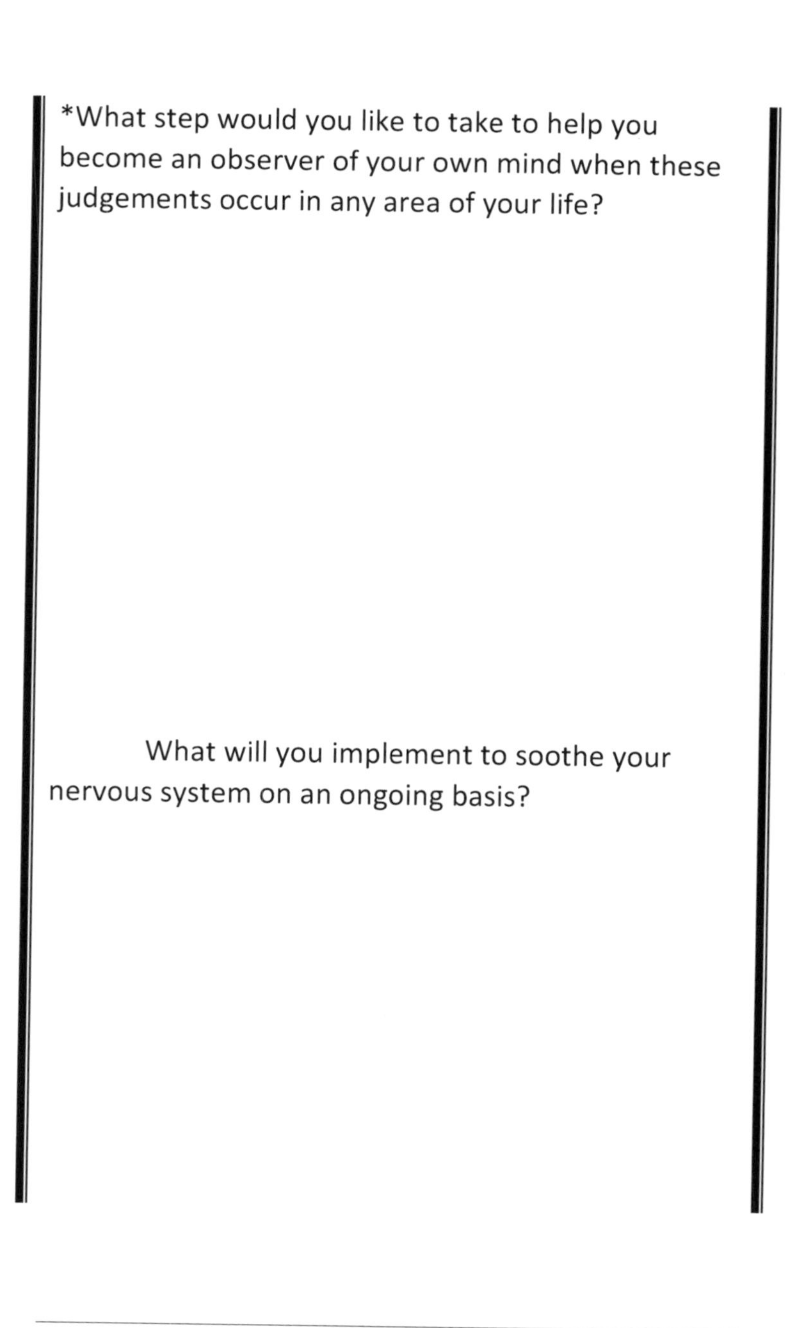

*What step would you like to take to help you become an observer of your own mind when these judgements occur in any area of your life?

What will you implement to soothe your nervous system on an ongoing basis?

DRAFTS, DISTRACTION AND DESPAIR

There is no correct way to draft work. Some people write in chronological order, others haphazardly wherever the story pulls them. Some write slowly, editing as they go. Others write in a fast, messy splurge to clean up later. And everything in between.

However, there may be some patterns to how you write that are indicative of broader patterns in your life. If they become problematic for you, it can be worth further investigation into the function and cost of these habitual ways of working. If they are not problematic for you, then there is no need to change them.

Let's focus on how ways of working can become traps.

Distraction and procrastination

It may be that working in bite-size chunks works well for you, to slowly but surely build a whole. However, there may be some examples of this pattern that are not about slow, steady progression of the tortoise versus the chaotic hare, but that in fact boil down to avoidance.

Watch out if your history tries to get you to label avoidance as laziness! Avoidance and procrastination are often an attempt at self-protection. That can be hard to understand when part of you is desperate to finish your writing. But think about all the potential risks that your mind may invent – will your writing disappoint you, will it disappoint others, is it too personal to share, have you felt pushed into writing something that isn't what your heart sings in order to increase the chance of publication? And quietly, oh, so quietly, you may have a mind that whispers, *you don't deserve success.*

Cover stories

One side effect of being a writer is that you may be skilled in telling yourself believable cover stories – so believable that you haven't noticed that's what they are. In order to avoid the 'riskiness' of writing, with all its imagined negative repercussions, you may construct excuses dressed as reasons. Take care to disentangle valid reasons for not writing from stories or excuses, and then to investigate what the function of avoidance is.

Rereading or chronic editing

There are many helpful aspects to rereading sections of previously written work while in the process of writing. Some people find an edit-as-you-go process to be motivating. But there comes a point at which this can tip into a form of avoidance with no way to move forwards. Some features of an unhelpful, chronic level of reading back or editing may be:

- A sense that you ‘need’ to keep rereading or editing, as if you can’t stop.
- Thoughts linked to not being able to produce something that matches this work or that it’s too poor to continue with.
- A sense of being stuck, as if rereading or editing constantly will somehow unlock the next steps, despite that not having worked the last fifty times.
- Past words feeling like a ‘safety net’ compared to a sense of dread at moving on from them.
- Feeling defeated, deflated or demotivated by the rereading or editing process but continuing to do it regardless.

Stuck in the middle

You may find a key point in writing where you feel completely stuck. Some writers say that is at the 30k mark in a novel, or after a short story is complete and there's the need to start developing a whole new world, or immediately after novel publication when they expected to be floating but find themselves flat on the floor instead. We can label such elements as 'second novel syndrome' or 'writer's block'. This feeling could be accompanied by lack of interest, flatness, numbness and/or disinterest. Others might experience heightened anxiety, inability to settle into writing, or a whirring mind that makes it difficult to focus.

*Consider the last time you experienced a sense of despair, complete lack of motivation, chronic rereading or re-editing, strong doubt or an urge to switch project. Which point in writing were you at then?

(e.g. after the excitement of the opening fades, at the midway point, as soon as you feel stuck, when you're overwhelmed with other stressors in life, when you read back over what you've written, after reading other writers' success)

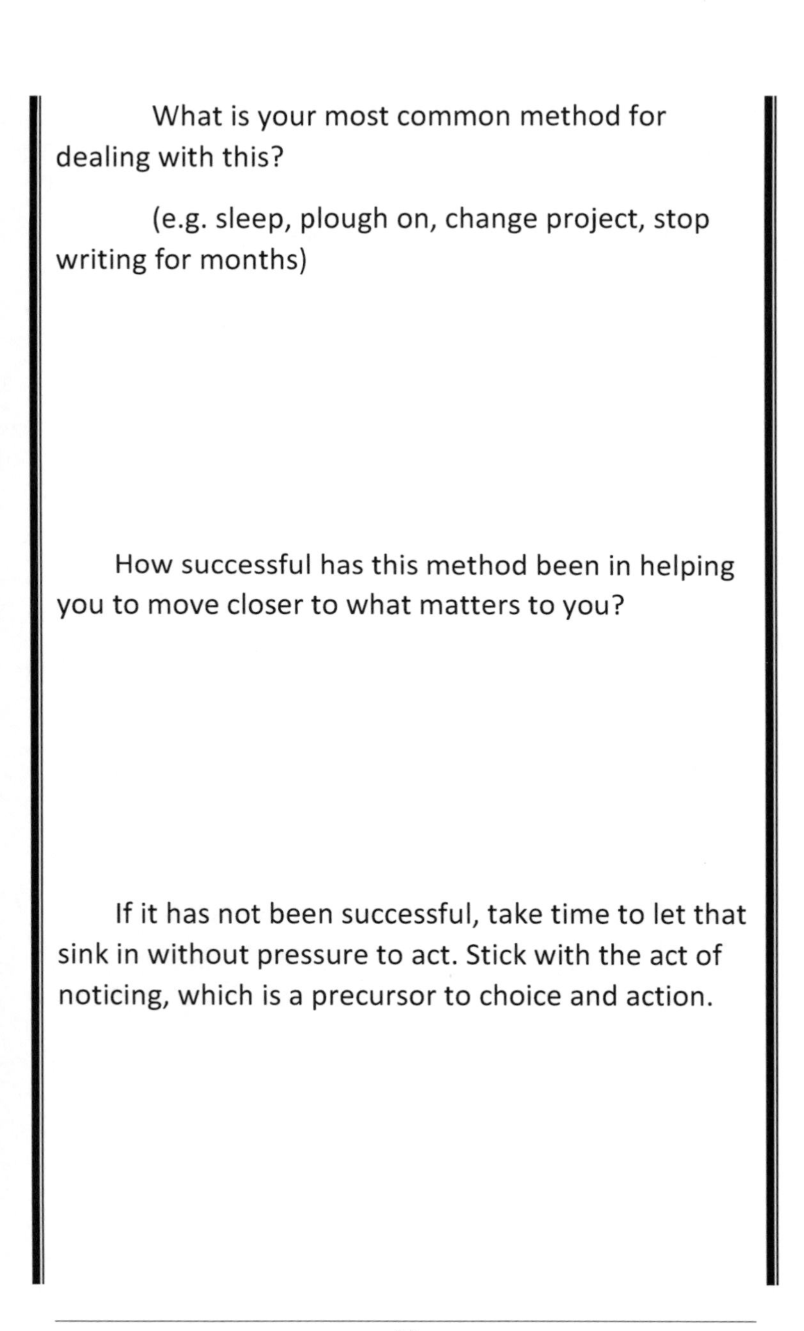

What is your most common method for dealing with this?

(e.g. sleep, plough on, change project, stop writing for months)

How successful has this method been in helping you to move closer to what matters to you?

If it has not been successful, take time to let that sink in without pressure to act. Stick with the act of noticing, which is a precursor to choice and action.

*If you have a tendency to try to 'push through' barriers with your writing but that has NOT been helpful, are there other areas in your life where you don't listen to your need for rest, play, relaxation, change, care from others, care for yourself?

What could you (or others) do to help you notice when you aren't listening to important messages from your body and mind?

What difference do you think this could make?

*If you have a tendency to avoid, procrastinate, change project frequently, or to tell yourself that you’re too busy with other priorities when that’s not the case, and this has NOT been helpful, is this a common pattern for you in other areas of life?

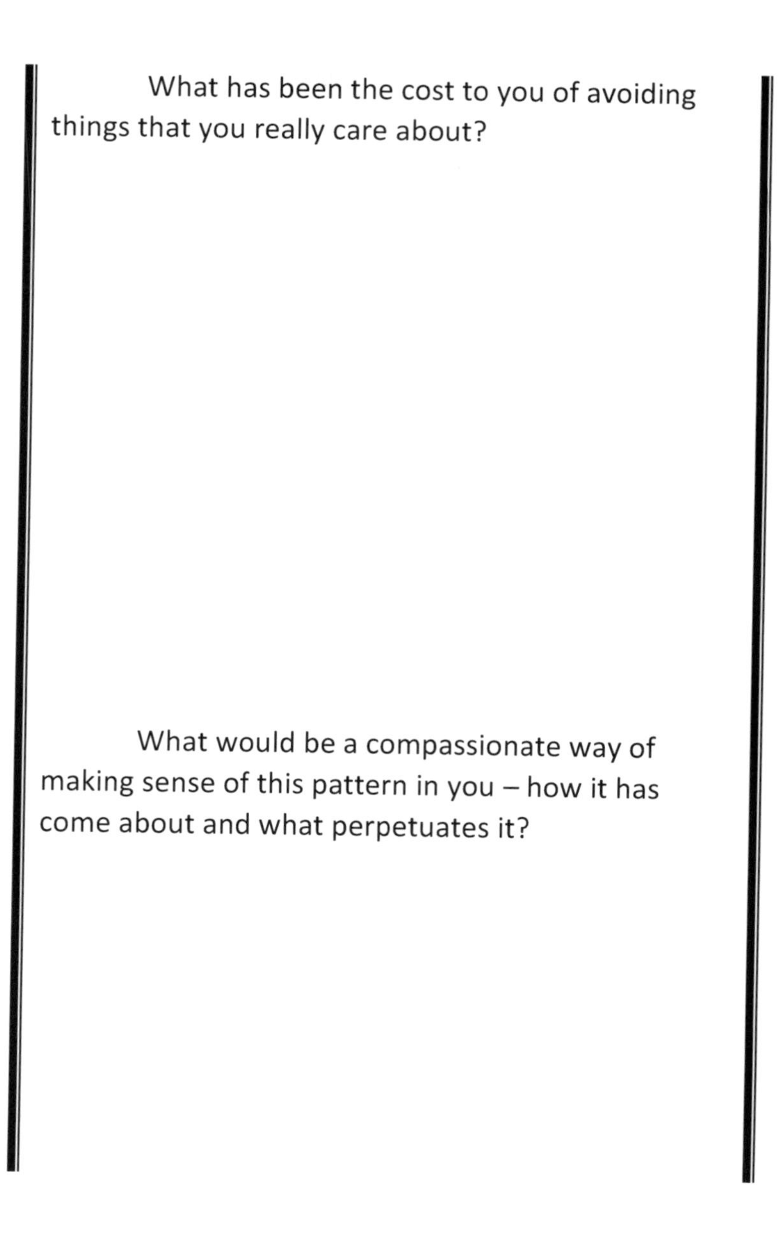

What has been the cost to you of avoiding things that you really care about?

What would be a compassionate way of making sense of this pattern in you – how it has come about and what perpetuates it?

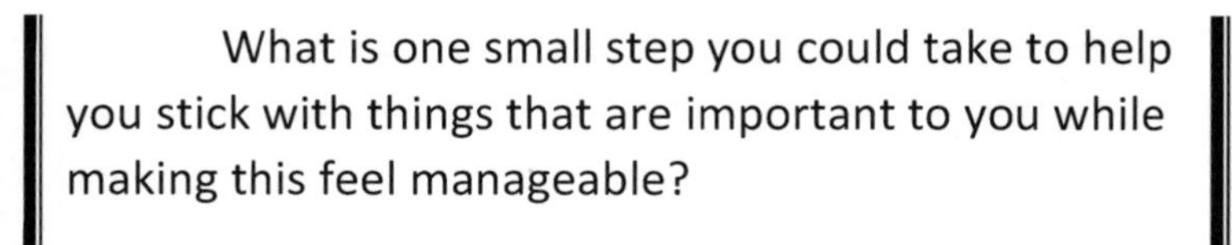

What is one small step you could take to help you stick with things that are important to you while making this feel manageable?

What would you hope the impact would be over the long term, if you reduced the amount of avoidance, procrastination or deprioritising?

DEADLINES

Are deadlines your friend or foe?

We have already reflected on the impact of our beliefs on how we feel and act. Now let's focus on your own relationship to deadlines to help you understand the role they play in your writing and what that might mean for you. It's unlikely you have a pattern that is the same every time, so hold these ideas lightly, but it may still be useful to look at the most common pattern for you.

One of the qualities of deadlines is that they are externally controlled. A competition closing date, a request from an editor or the window for submissions of a magazine provide an external structure. If you take a moment to focus on a specific deadline, you can tune in to what sensations, emotions or thoughts arise. For example:

COMPETITION – pressure – foggy head – *'There's no point trying'*

EDITOR – anxiety – feel sick – *'I can't let her down'*

SUBMISSION – exciting – energised – *'I don't want to miss out'*

You can also create your own deadlines. Do they hold the same sway? They might start to feel oppressive, in which case we're more likely to avoid or rail against them. Some writers set themselves up to fail by creating unrealistic deadlines, which then add further pressure and intensify beliefs of not being good enough. Are you using your internal deadlines as a tool or as a weapon?

Whatever your relationship is with deadlines, you can change this over time. Remember, you're more likely to enter a state of flow with some degree of challenge but not by being overwhelmed.

*What is your relationship with deadlines?

Paralysing or energising?

A means of avoidance in the present moment or an end date to plan towards?

Externally driven as a 'must' or internally driven as 'I want to'?

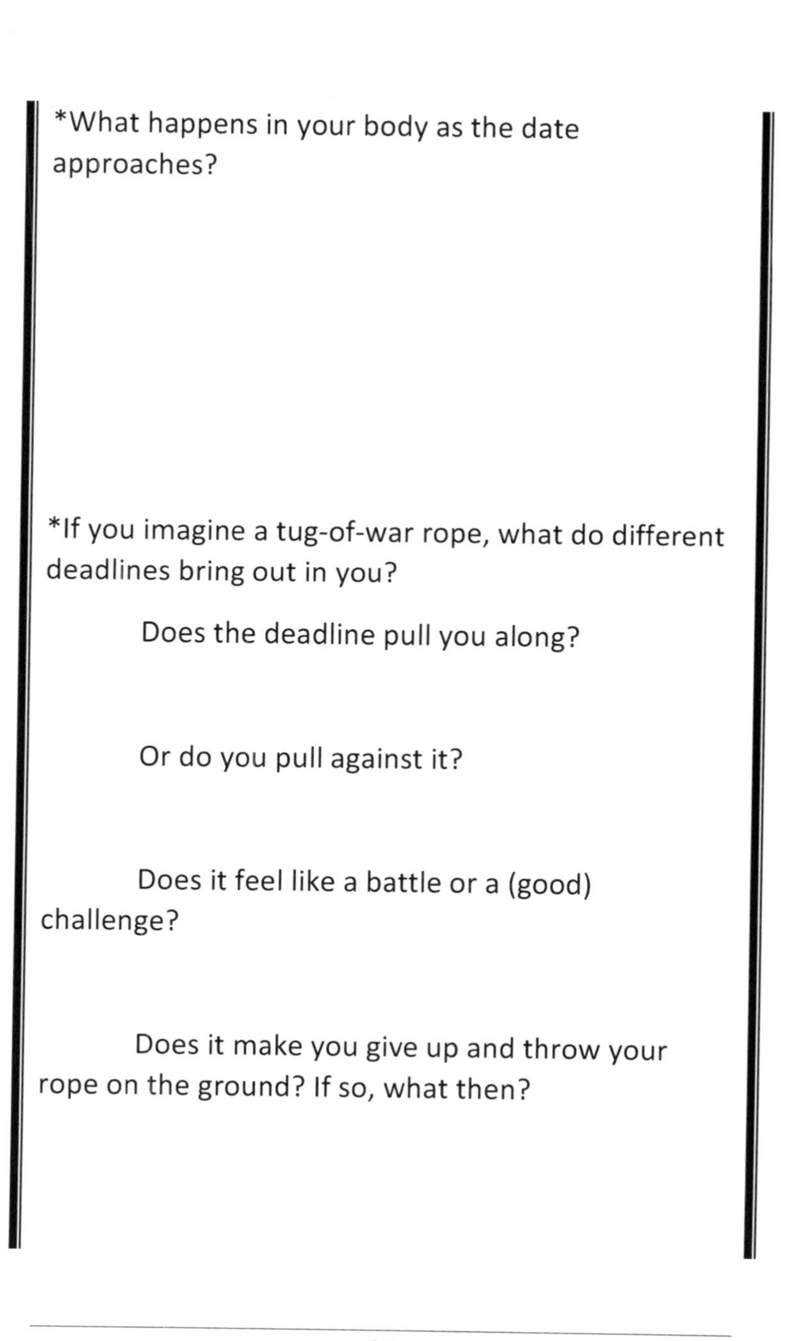

*What happens in your body as the date approaches?

*If you imagine a tug-of-war rope, what do different deadlines bring out in you?

Does the deadline pull you along?

Or do you pull against it?

Does it feel like a battle or a (good) challenge?

Does it make you give up and throw your rope on the ground? If so, what then?

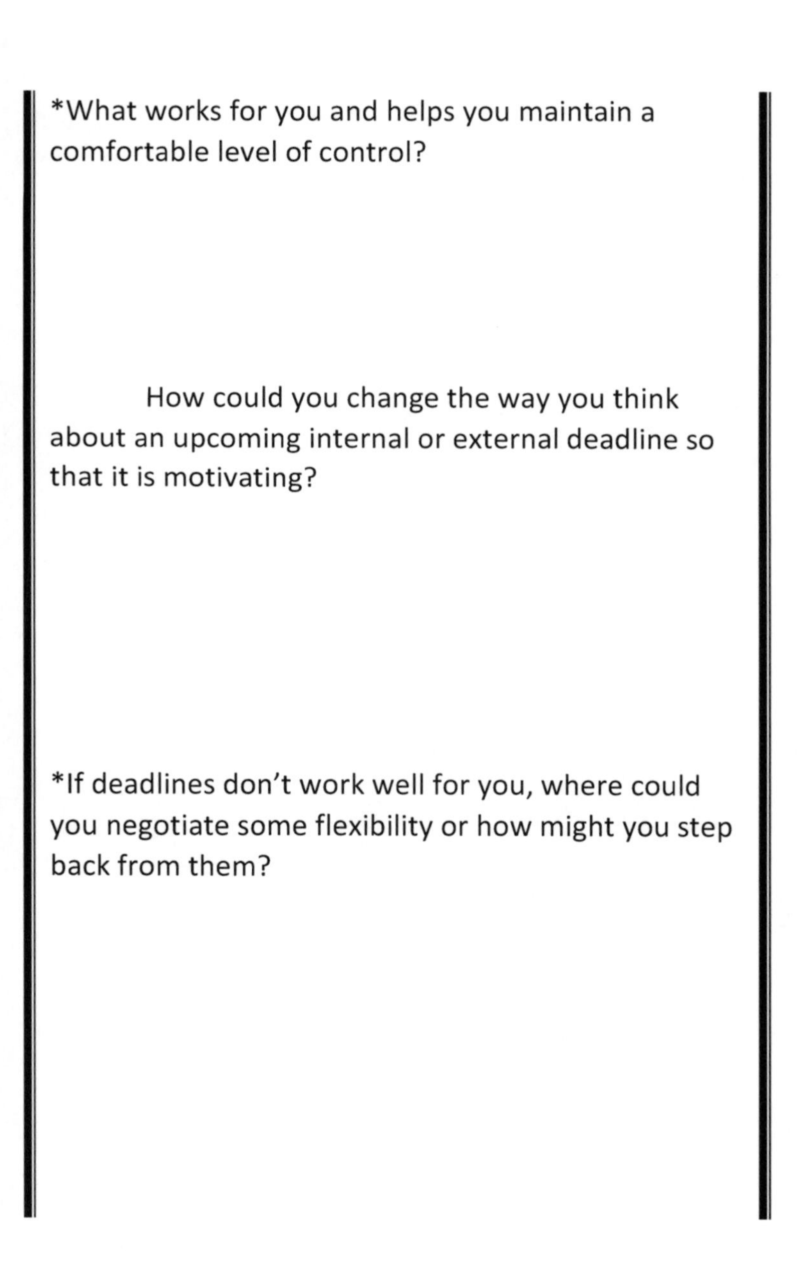

*What works for you and helps you maintain a comfortable level of control?

How could you change the way you think about an upcoming internal or external deadline so that it is motivating?

*If deadlines don't work well for you, where could you negotiate some flexibility or how might you step back from them?

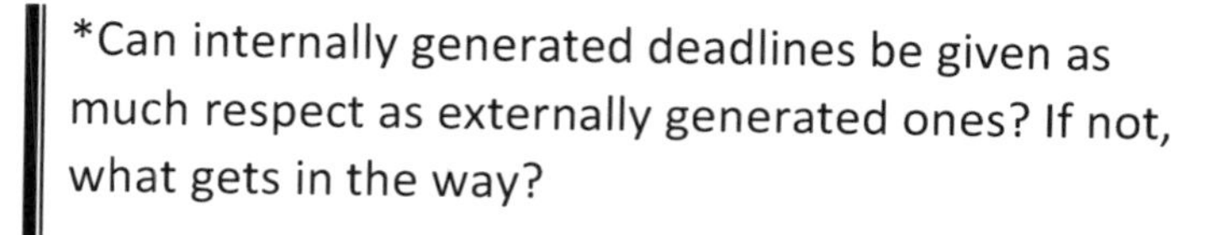

*Can internally generated deadlines be given as much respect as externally generated ones? If not, what gets in the way?

*Do you see other parts of your life where these patterns play out? How have you dealt with those?

*Think back, perhaps, to your earlier life and your relationship with deadlines such as homework or tasks set in the home to help you reflect on where your relationship with deadlines comes from and how that has developed over time.

Perfection or Good Enough

Perfectionism

Perhaps you describe yourself as a 'perfectionist' or recognise those tendencies. What do we mean by this and how does it impact on your writing process?

Perfectionism is the tendency to set excessively high standards for yourself and it can be divided into two forms, which are not mutually exclusive. (You are invited to view these terms with curiosity rather than use them as a device to judge yourself or tie yourself down.) Adaptive perfectionism is characterised by a striving for achievement with the ability to tolerate small mistakes, while maladaptive perfectionism involves highly critical self-evaluations with little or no tolerance for error.[20]

In terms of the process of writing, writers with adaptive perfectionism are more likely to use self-criticism to propel themselves forward, whereas those with maladaptive perfectionism are more focused on avoiding error and, as such, are more likely to procrastinate as an avoidance strategy. If you can only bear throwing sixes, you might stop rolling the dice altogether.

Perfectionism can also differ in terms of where the focus lies, whether in self-imposed standards or socially prescribed to gain others' approval.[21]

As multifaceted as perfectionism is, in it lies a risk that such high standards impact on the writing process and sense of satisfaction with what is written.

If you have perfectionist tendencies, it's likely that their thorned roses show themselves across different domains of your life. It can be tricky to separate out different factors such as tenacity, fighting against a system that oppresses or fails to support you, determination, passion and diligence from a pattern of perfectionism that can be punitive and that might strip you of satisfaction (outside of high achievement).

*Do either of the definitions of perfectionism resonate for you in your writing life?

*Would you like to consider the origins of this? You could write it as memoir, fictionalise it or create a fake diary entry from when the perfectionism emerged.

*If you tend to 'push' yourself to succeed, what could you put in place to prevent that pattern tipping you into excessive self-criticism and all its fallout? What are the warning signs?

*If you find yourself avoiding finishing or submitting work and suspect this is due to intense fear of not being perfect (or of rejection), what steps could you put in place to prioritise play and feeling safe with your writing in the short term?

Who could help with this?

'Making do'

If perfectionism doesn't chime for you, perhaps your pattern of thinking tells you what you've just completed 'will do' and you quickly move on from it before it is polished. You may tell yourself that it's better to keep trying different things rather than get bogged down on one idea, or that the chances of publication are low, so you don't want to overinvest in one project, or that the writing is only for your own satisfaction. 'I threw my hat in the ring at the last minute', 'this isn't my best', 'I'm just practising what it feels like to submit' and so on. The act of avoiding 'aiming high' brings its own protection: if the work isn't accepted, shortlisted, read or published or doesn't sell well, you can tell yourself that it didn't matter anyway, it wasn't your full effort. This way, your brain is cocooned to some extent from the sense of rejection it dreads. But is it worth the price of missing out on the satisfaction and possibilities that your best work could bring?

*If you think you under-invest in your writing, for example by not giving it sufficient editing time, how might you stop and notice that as it happens?

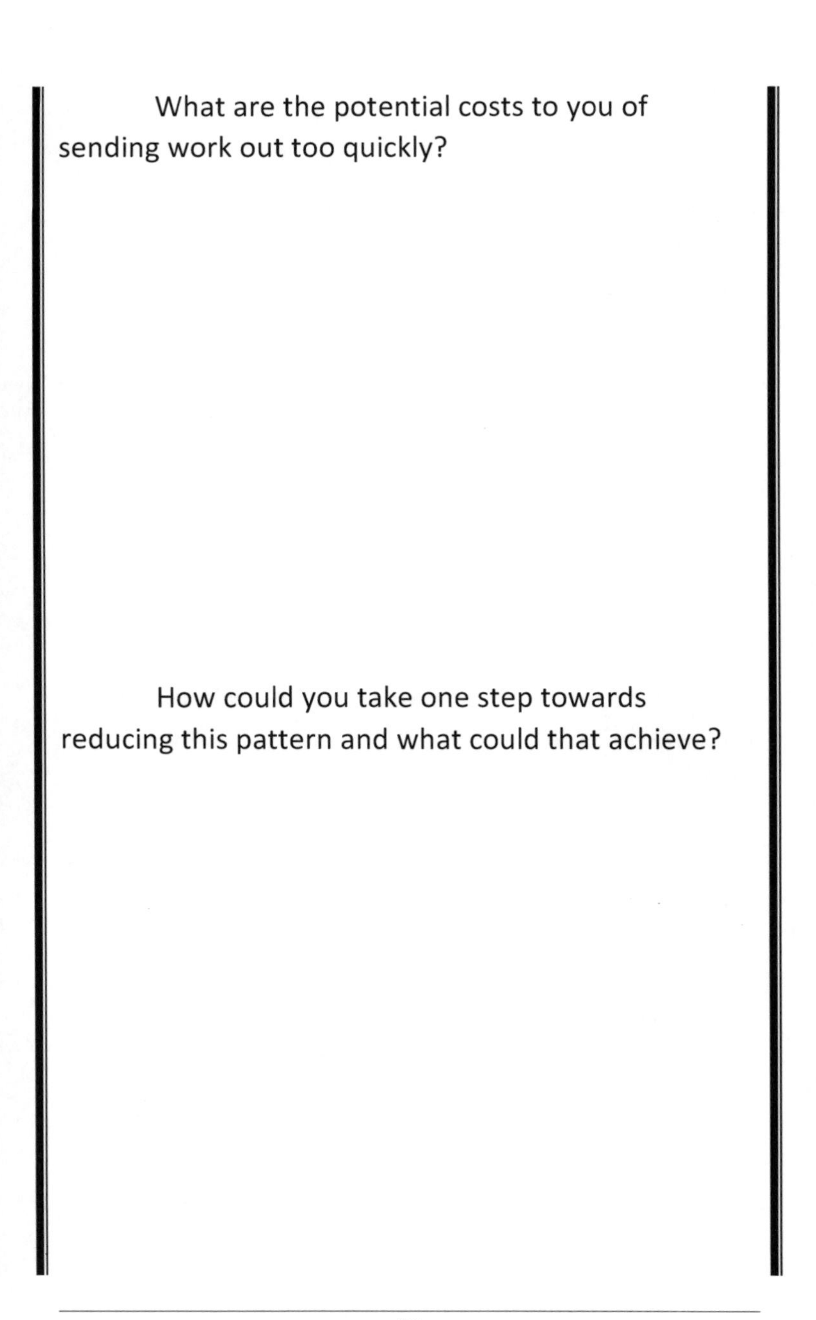

What are the potential costs to you of sending work out too quickly?

How could you take one step towards reducing this pattern and what could that achieve?

*On your next writing project, or something else important to you that you're trying to achieve, consider the difference between saying 'it will do' versus actual satisfaction, without it tipping over into perfectionism.

What would each of these states feel like?

*What are your memories about feeling judged or failing at things earlier in your life?

Can you think of times you had to protect yourself with the armour of speed or trying not to care?

With compassion, can you write to your younger or current self with some advice regarding the current use of this pattern, now you can see it had a function at an earlier time?

Part 2: Content

What you write

THEMES

Common themes

Writers are sometimes asked to reflect on common themes in their work. By acting as a researcher of yourself, you can conduct an analysis of the content of your work at different layers.

We will start with a review of WHAT you tend to write. For those of you who write fiction, it can be helpful to pull back and look at qualities, themes, relationships and dynamics within and between your characters. On the surface, two characters in separate projects may seem as if they have nothing in common. However, if you strip away the more superficial aspects, you might discover a thread between them.

Let's say a writer has published a children's book that focuses on Lottie's quests in a dreamworld – a fun, wholesome adventure story. With an interest in branching out, this writer jotted down notes for an adult thriller in which a nurse called Pip has to play detective to uncover what her colleagues are really up to. There are no surface-level similarities between the two main characters. But then the writer decides to investigate by digging a layer deeper. She answers some questions for both characters and finds although there are differences, the following characteristics are present in both:

- What is the character's strength?
  Tenacity, empathy, sense of duty
- What do they care about?
  Other people, making a difference
- How do they relate to others?
  Try to bring out the best in them
  What surprises others about them in the story?
  She shows more courage than expected in dangerous circumstances in order to do the right thing
- What changes in them over the arc?
  She speaks her mind more, acknowledges her own strengths

It is not a problem if you find – or don't find – such similarities. The purpose of the exercise is to help you reflect on the patterns and meaning-making of your work and ideas.

What types of characters do you tend to focus on? Try asking questions about the characters as in the example above, or create a list to summarise commonalities.

(e.g. loners, people under pressure, bullies, underdogs, those who have survived an atrocity, people with a secret)

Did you find any similarities that you hadn't noticed before?

Next, you can take a wider look at your body of work to see what you tend to be pulled towards in your writing or what is in your 'comfort zone'. The suggestions below aren't clear dichotomies in real writing but they do allow you to consider where on the scale your writing tends to sit. You might prefer to separate out different writing projects if they are poles apart, such as memoir and science fiction.

*Review your previous writing, or ideas you've had that are not yet written, and decide where most fall. You can just give a score or write a brief description of where your work sits for each opposite pair.

Where does your work tend to sit on the following:

POSITIVE – NEGATIVE / DARK

HUMOROUS – SERIOUS

POETIC – PLAIN LANGUAGE

COMFORTING – DISCOMFORTING FOR READER

CHRONOLOGICAL – OUT OF SEQUENCE

CLEAR STORY / MEANING – MYSTERIOUS / OPEN TO INTERPRETATION

REALISM – MAGICAL / WEIRD

RELATES TO MY LIFE – NOT AT ALL MY LIFE

MORE FOCUSED ON STORY – MORE FOCUSED ON CHARACTER

RESOLVED ENDING – UNRESOLVED / AMBIGUOUS ENDING

*Do these patterns match your deliberate intention or does the writing just seem to 'come out' that way?

*Work your way through the pairs with non-judgemental curiosity, seeing if you can hypothesise WHY you write this way. There may be some that you can attach clear reasons to (e.g. advised by agent or what you prefer to read) and some that are harder to answer (which may be hidden away in your unconscious mind).

Now you can pay attention to what you DON'T or rarely write – it can be hard to know what isn't there in your work until you are prompted to notice the gaps.

*In each pair, review the pole that you don't tend to use, for example if you never write stories in chronological order or never include magical elements. List them. Then pay attention to your reaction to each.

Are there any on the 'not me' list that create a strong reaction, either against or toward?

Are you happy with your chosen focus or do you feel the urge to push a little in a new direction? If so, how will you do this in a playful, safe way?

Avoidance and hidden gems

What we avoid writing may also tell us something. It could be that we have little interest or experience in these gaps. But we could also be sitting on a rich mine of experience that we are unconsciously avoiding. It's not the case that you ought to write in ways that are opposite to your usual tendencies, but it may be enlightening to consider why you don't.

Why would our minds do this censoring? Sometimes, as self-protection. There could be some unconscious resistance: a part of your mind that wishes to keep you away from its associations that are particular to you. Or the censorship could be tied in with your unconscious yearnings, disallowed and pushed to the bottom of the ocean of your awareness

You don't need to dive in to what has been pushed down or disallowed. However, you might find that the first step to creating writing based on this rich, buried treasure comes from having choice: you can't choose to address a gap if you don't realise it's there.

Let's take some examples of incidences where you can't explain the gap by practical means (e.g. agent says this doesn't sell, I'm not interested in stories like this) or obvious emotional means (I am choosing to avoid this as it reminds me of something or someone difficult):

If your characters always have a gloomy arc, then one area you are missing involves tales of redemption and success. Perhaps there is an unconscious censoring going on here, as if redemption and/or success are not what you deserve or these elements bring you too close to some yearning.

If you write about big themes in life but notice that death or loss are missing, perhaps that's an avoided area due to pain or fear.

If you are drawn to dynamics between siblings or parent and child but rarely partners, then you've found another gap that may touch on something painful from the past or a yearning that you're avoiding without realising.

To be clear, we all have our preferences, and there's nothing wrong with that. Nor is there any rule that says you SHOULD write about the other things. But look through your list of typical characters and table of writing patterns. What comes up when you consider your gaps? If you experience a reaction inside your body or a strong pull to look away from – or an itch to revisit – a 'gap', maybe you have an untold story to explore here. Whether you do explore or not is your choice. But this process can help you pay attention to what is currently 'pushed down' inside your unconscious. It may feel impossible to write, or you may find it starts to pour out once you make it about a fictional character rather than yourself.

*Are there any links between what you avoid in your writing that seem relevant to the rest of your life?

If so, is this a sensible protection you wish to acknowledge but leave to one side for now? Or would you like to spend some reflective time by yourself or with a trusted other to think or write it through?

REPETITION

Our writing can be a communication to others, and also to ourselves.

Word and sound repetition

You can find free websites that allow you to paste in chunks of your writing to analyse word frequency. There will be common words that you expect to see repeated. However, you may find some more unusual or unexpected words that form part of the fingerprint of your work. Or, going forward and back through new and old writing, you may notice a frequently used unusual word or repeated image. When you edit, you might insert the perfect word... only to find it two sentences later.

There are probably words you are drawn to for various reasons: a shared understanding of implied meaning, a word particular to your place of birth or culture, the shape or length of a word that fits your style, sensory aspects that are pleasing to write or that you believe will evoke a certain reaction in the reader, for example. There may even be letters or sounds you particularly enjoy or are pulled towards.

Our brains are wired for connection. That is to say, even a single sound or word can evoke memories and emotion, and influence behaviour.

Let's say I tell you to pay attention to a long *sssssss* sound. Does it evoke a memory of the snake in the film *The Jungle Book*, or the deflation of a balloon after a party when a child is left alone, or is it sensuous, as if close to your ear, or the start of somebody's name that you love or fear?

Word choices are not neutral, and writers often select carefully those descriptors that match the 'voice' of a character or the heart of a poem. But there are likely to be times when a word is selected for a reason that is not immediately obvious to the writer.

Wider elements of repetition

Moving wider than word choice, the lens through which you write, and where you focus, may help you notice what is important to you and what you tend to avoid. If sense of smell plays a significant role for you, perhaps your stories are more likely to repeat words such as vanilla, sniff, petrol or petrichor.

Paying attention to what lens you tend to write through can aid self-awareness. It could be that your writing tells you about your sense of self and state of mind at the time you wrote a particular paragraph or poem, in a way you hadn't realised at the time.

For example, do your poems contain repeated imagery of sharp objects or precise word choices at key points with sharp sounds and edges? Does your prose keep returning to a theme of lost love or overcoming adversity?

Repetition can signal a need to pay attention. It could be a warning, a guide or a chance to reconnect with hidden yearnings or past pain.

*Using whichever method you prefer, try to identify repetitions such as:

Colour

Objects

Words or sounds

Metaphors

Body parts

Breath

Movement

Danger

Hope

Sensory detail

Moral or message

*Which of the above strike you as relevant as you read through your answers?

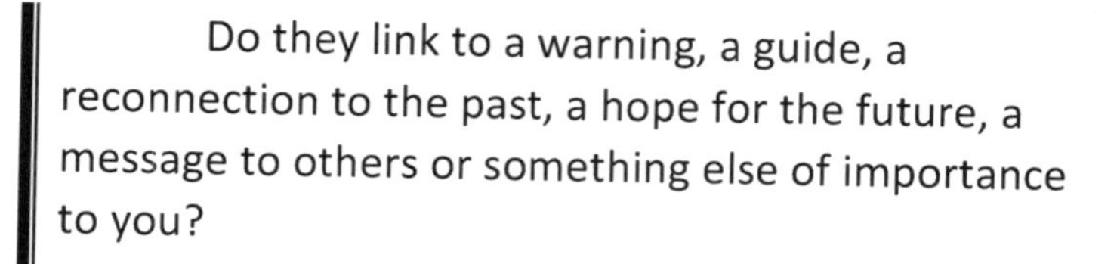

Do they link to a warning, a guide, a reconnection to the past, a hope for the future, a message to others or something else of importance to you?

What have you learned from this exercise about your writing or yourself?

EMOTIONS

Range of emotions

What kind of emotional world you create in your writing also links to the emotional responses of the reader – sometimes in expected ways, other times in surprising ways, as their own history, context and mindset interact with your intentions. But how might this world relate to your own emotions?

You may have noticed how your own feelings during writing impact upon the content that emerges. Or perhaps you purposefully have tried to write from an emotional perspective very different to yours at the time, taking on a cloak of happiness, grief or rage. But that cloak was waiting in the wardrobe for you, as a person who has undoubtedly experienced the full range of feelings over the course of time.

Acceptability of emotions

Throughout our lives, each of us receives messages about which emotions are *acceptable.* However, emotions are in fact innate, as demonstrated when babies display the core emotions such as sadness at separation, fear of the unfamiliar, anger at not being fed immediately. As children grow, the outward signs of some of these emotions may be encouraged or reinforced while others are discouraged, ignored or punished. Further information from school, media, and wider society shapes how emotions are expressed and which ones may become exaggerated (e.g. *being angry and acting aggressively keeps me safe*) or suppressed (e.g. *crying makes me vulnerable or a burden*).

Suppressing emotions for a long time can lead to them becoming *repressed* – that is, the individual is not aware of the presence of the emotion.

The emotional content of writing is not only character-based. Imagery, language choice, setting, description, storyline and many other elements create an emotional atmosphere.

Let's take a look at key emotions in your writing.

*Use one main piece of work to complete the questions below:

Emotions shown by main characters

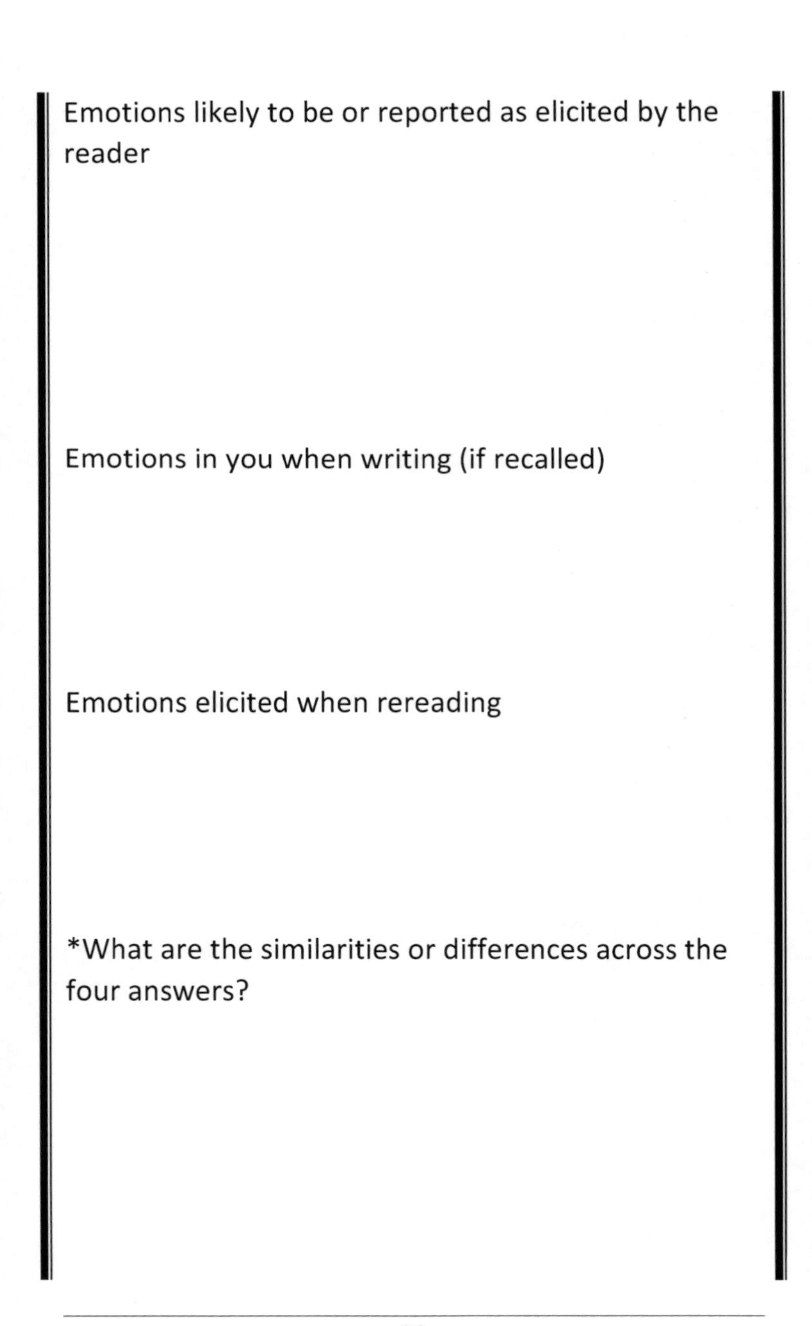

Emotions likely to be or reported as elicited by the reader

Emotions in you when writing (if recalled)

Emotions elicited when rereading

*What are the similarities or differences across the four answers?

*How ‘in touch’ do you feel with the main emotions found in your characters or readers?

If you don’t feel in touch at all, do you notice any sense of unease, numbness or tightening in the throat, as if something is trying to rise up, or a desire to avoid that could signal these emotions have somehow been pushed down for you?

*What is important to you about showing or eliciting emotions via your writing?

Expressing emotional content

Writing can have therapeutic benefits that lead to changes in physical and mental health. This is particularly true of 'expressive' writing which involves emotionally laden rather than emotionally neutral content,[22] An exploration of your own patterns regarding emotions, and how these may or may not be reflected in your writing, will give you a greater understanding of the inter-relationship between the two.

*As you write, do you take care of your own emotional world?

*In your daily life, do you pay attention to, take care of, allow and normalise your emotional world?

Pay attention to those emotions that are not present on your list as well as those that are.

*What are some ways that will enable you to maximise the helpful impact of writing on your emotional life (e.g. as release, exploration, sharing) and minimise any harm (e.g. feeling overwhelmed, tipped into numbness or forced to share intimate details).

RESIDUE

Residue is what remains after a process is completed. When you finish reading a novel or watching a film, you might find that while you can't describe it as a whole, specific details remain. This may be a cognitive experience – a memory of a specific image or a line spoken by a character. Or it could be on a more bodily level, such as being left with a sense of uneasiness or lightness.

Reflecting on residue

These fragments are meaningful in some way. They may tap into something at a conscious or unconscious level (or both). If you're interested in understanding what some layers of your writing mean, you could pay attention to what 'sticks' during the process of planning, writing, editing or rereading your work.

When you look back at previous story ideas, abandoned projects or completed works, they may have something new to show you. You can access this by purposefully recalling that piece and seeing what small elements emerge from the hazy memory of it, or by rereading them and seeing what comes to mind later as you lie in bed or stand in the shower.

The photosensitive cells in our eyes differ. The cones are found in the centre of the retina and are responsible for vision in bright light. The rods are situated on the edge of the retina and aid vision in dim lighting such as at night. So, if you want to see something in a darkened room, your vision works best if you use a sideways glance rather than staring directly. Like with night vision, in our writing it can sometimes be helpful to not stare too hard at what we are trying to see. By taking time away from our own work, we can pay attention to what emerges in thoughts or images and decide whether these are the fragments worth reflecting on.

*Read back over your earliest work or plans related to writing, trying to resist judging it. Allow curiosity. Focus on images, scenes, a key phrase or line in a poem. What stands out in the moment and what sticks a few days later?

What impact does this particular fragment have on your mood and body?

If this impact was a message to you from your own mind, what would it say? (e.g. *explore more on this topic, this still hurts, beauty is important, I have something to say*)

*Look at a small chunk from a current, or your most recent, piece of writing or planning. If you had to summarise the piece, its imagery or the feelings it invokes in only three words, what would they be? (*e.g. jealousy, strength, glowing*)

Use the three words as prompts for a totally new piece of free-writing (that is, without planning: just write) to see where that takes you.

Are these words meaningful to you from any other areas of life?

In what ways?

Take the time to notice any urges to act or avoid when you focus on these words. What does that tell you?

DIFFERENCE AND POWER

As mentioned in the previous chapter, our internal experiences of ourselves, others and the world spill out onto the page. Even when we deliberately write from a point of view or experience different from our own, that writing can still only come via our own mind and therefore it is filtered in ways we don't realise.

We live in an unjust world where power and influence are unfairly distributed. The chances are that throughout your life there have been times you've felt powerless, unheard or as though you were different. You might have had multiple disadvantages, arising from the context in which you've grown up in and/or live now, which define how safe or appropriate you have felt or feel in expressing certain thoughts. There could also be situations and relationships when you've been part of the majority or held power.

Look at the dynamics between characters in your writing. By writing from different points of view in fiction and poetry, you might already have explored all these roles: the powerful and the powerless, those who fit into the mainstream and those who don't.

When parts of us feel cut off, misunderstood or silenced, writing can be a way of gaining a voice. We may also benefit from acknowledging and exploring the discomfort we feel at ways in which we are privileged, via a less threatening format of creative writing.

*What power dynamics play out in your stories?

Are there ways in which any of your characters are 'outsiders' or fail to be heard or understood?

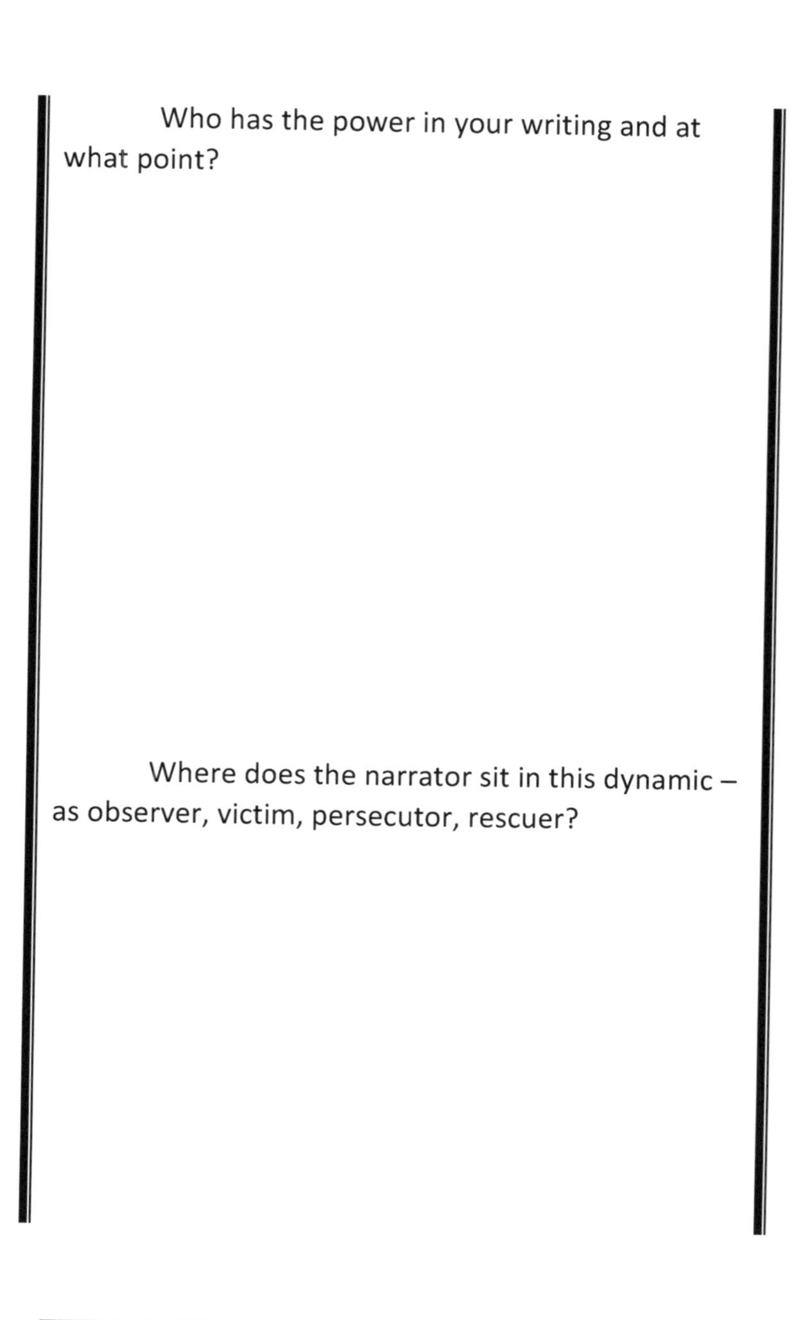

Who has the power in your writing and at what point?

Where does the narrator sit in this dynamic – as observer, victim, persecutor, rescuer?

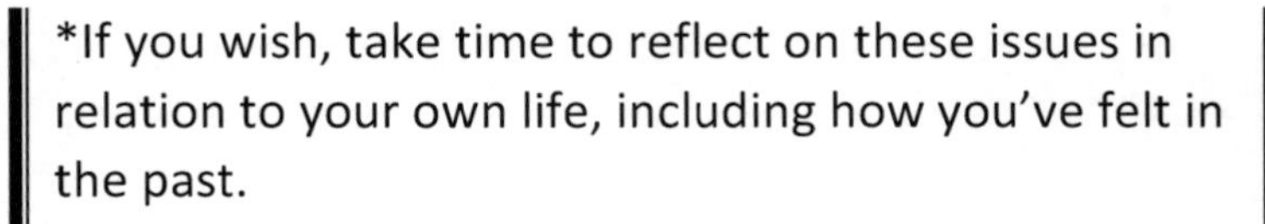

*If you wish, take time to reflect on these issues in relation to your own life, including how you've felt in the past.

Are any of the roles familiar to you or people close to you from the past or present?

Notice if and how your writing explores the impact of power differences, who you've given voice or hope to, what the arc is for characters.

Think about your current circumstances and the ways in which you hold power or dominance and any ways in which you are marginalised, mistreated, powerless or feel the need to tread carefully due to power imbalances.

Are there parts of you that don't feel seen, understood or allowed to be expressed?

Are there any ways in which the act of writing gives you opportunity to challenge injustice, rebalance power or have voices heard that are usually stifled, in a way that's meaningful to you?

What does this task bring up for you? Allow yourself room to notice while taking care of yourself.

YEARNINGS

During the chapter on themes, we touched on the idea of yearning in both the characters and the author. Let's investigate further.

Yearnings in characters

In fiction and memoir, the character usually wants something. For example, they want to save the planet, solve the crime, win a prize or get justice. If you excavate below the surface-level desire, you can find further meaning. A character who wants to save the planet could actually be trying to right a past wrong, or believes that only something so momentous would make them loveable. The *yearning* behind the desire or behaviour can be hidden from the characters themselves, sometimes revealing itself over the story arc.

Eliciting yearning in the reader and self

In poetry and some prose, the 'yearning' of the story could be said to lie in what it tries to evoke in the reader, such as nostalgia for childhood and what has been lost, a sense of the beauty in the smallest element of nature, a sense of connectedness to others.

In this context, you can consider the 'yearning' within your writing to be the deepest desire for something meaningful, such as to be cherished, recognised, heard, loved, part of a greater whole, accepted, authentic, forgiven, with a sense of belonging.

By exploring yearning in your writing, you can also explore any mirrors to yearning within yourself. The behaviour could look very different in a character than in ourselves, while mirroring the same underlying theme.

*What yearnings lie beneath the behaviour of your characters, or what yearnings might your writing evoke in your reader?

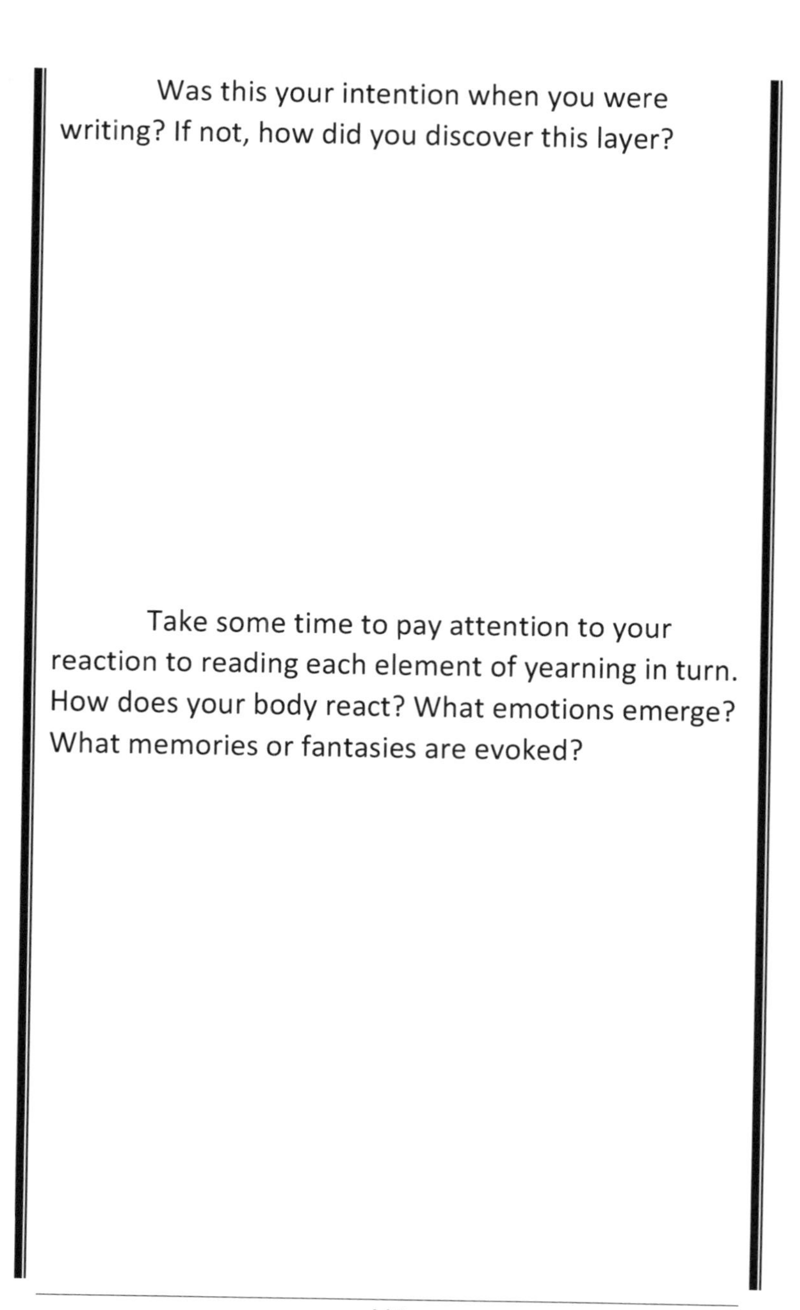

Was this your intention when you were writing? If not, how did you discover this layer?

Take some time to pay attention to your reaction to reading each element of yearning in turn. How does your body react? What emotions emerge? What memories or fantasies are evoked?

If you slow down and pay quiet attention, do any of these yearnings resonate as being meaningful to you? If so, is that acknowledged in how you live your life?

*If you'd like to explore further, think about whether there are ways in which your core needs are not being met and how this shows up in your writing?

What first step could you take to address this?

Part 3: Discovery

Writing life

Language about Writing

Impact of language choices

The language we use about our writing impacts on how we think and feel about it. It shapes the perception of our world and our expectations. Specific words each have their own implications and associated references. When you look at words in a thesaurus, you will see they are not actually interchangeable – each resonates in a different way and is selected for a certain purpose.

Let's consider the implications of some common phrases related to writing.

The phrase 'shitty first draft' appears to have the purpose of taking the pressure off writers to aim for perfection. But if you were to write this phrase in the centre of a page and create a mind map of associated words and images, what would that word 'shitty' lead off to? That's what happens in your brain: a form of mind-mapping where related words, images and memories are nudged with each use of a word. There may well be benefits to this phrase, but it might pay to be mindful of unintended consequences and the impact on creativity, behaviour and mood. You could end up feeling... well, shitty.

Another common phrase is 'writer's block'. What images does that elicit? A boulder, barricade, immovable object? If you focus inwards, where in your body can you 'feel' that phrase? A constriction, blockage, closed-throat sensation, perhaps? Or does it feel like a non-threatening image of a temporary pause, such as a large orange cone in the road that is present for a short time while important maintenance work takes place? What is the likely impact of these different images on your sense of freedom, creativity, mood, motivation? Word and image choices are not neutral.

Language choice regarding our writer-self

Moving on to how we describe our writing and ourselves, what does the word 'wannabe' or 'aspiring' writer elicit for you? Remember – there is no right or wrong here! For one writer, 'aspire' might feel full of hope, on the precipice of something worth working for. For another, it could be devaluing or reduce energy, reawakening an old sense of not being good enough or ready yet, which then impacts upon behaviour.

How about 'award-winning' or 'bestseller'? Does that evoke pride and motivation, or does it make you feel under threat and likely to fail to live up to high expectations?

How does your language position you? For example, a writer who announces a shortlisting in a writing competition by stating they 'snuck onto' the list. What are you saying about yourself with the language you use to share news or progress?

It is helpful to pay attention to our histories with specific words. One word is tethered to another, so that *proud* could be tethered to the word *arrogant*, which brings up certain emotions and memories; or *proud* could be tethered to a memory of warm affection and regard, leading to motivation and appreciation towards the self.

As you become more mindful of the words you automatically use about writing and your writer-self, and the impact of them, you are likely to also notice the language you use about other aspects of your life. Treat yourself kindly. You are stepping into self-knowledge and wisdom; there is no need to attack yourself for accidentally adding to your own undermining by using certain words or phrases habitually

By opening your eyes to these word patterns as habits, you have the power to choose, rehearse and embed new ones.

*What do you call a first draft?

Is it a helpful or neutral phrase? What emerges if you write this phrase in the centre of the page and see what words, other phrases or images come from it?

*Over the next few weeks, pay attention to the language you use with others and in your own mind around your own writing and yourself.

What is the impact of this language in each situation?

Does your evidence suggest any words that could be used more or less?

Can you plan some new words or phrases to use in specific situations (e.g. when someone asks what you do for a living; when you describe your current work-in-progress)?

*Are any of your self-labelling patterns a problem in other aspects of your life?

Pay attention to the words you use to describe your appearance, age, roles, etc. Do they trap you into a certain way of being or feeling? If you notice one that you're not satisfied with, with practice, you can replace it.

Relationship with Writing

It may seem peculiar to consider something outside of human contact as a 'relationship'. But if you are willing to be playful, let's consider our relationship to our own writing in this way.

Our minds create a template of how we fit into the world in different situations. It is easy to fall into repeating patterns of relating without intending to. (In cases where this is based on difficult early experiences, this is called the repetition compulsion.[23])

Your relationship with writing could be explored in different ways, such as a dance, a marriage or a family relationship, or as if it is a work relationship where who plays the role of boss fluctuates.

Our relationships change over time. Consider a friend you've known for a long time. Were there periods when you were closer, had more in common or no longer seemed on the same wavelength? The changes in a romantic relationship can span from obsession to hatred and everything in between, just as writing can at one point be all-consuming and at another something you hide from with contempt.

Part of how relationships function relates to beliefs, expectations and the roles that each person falls into. This is where patterns can recur.

*What kind of friend or foe can writing be at different times?

*Choose a way to consider your relationship with writing: a dance, a romantic partner, a friendship, a family member, a work relationship or any other relationship that seems relevant.

What dynamics play out in this relationship? You can write or draw this out.

Notice what language and images emerge when you think of your writing this way, for example as a fair-weather friend, a punishing boss, a secret lover.

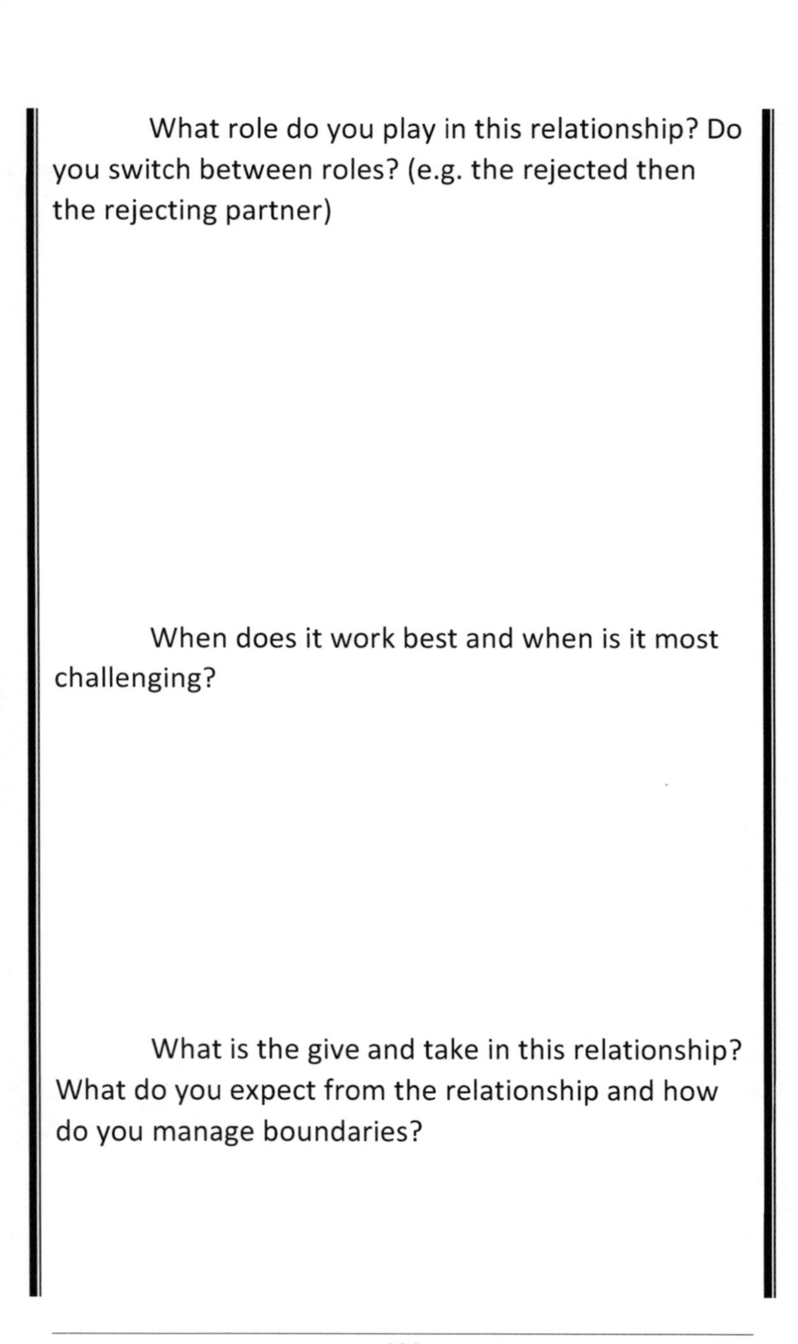

What role do you play in this relationship? Do you switch between roles? (e.g. the rejected then the rejecting partner)

When does it work best and when is it most challenging?

What is the give and take in this relationship? What do you expect from the relationship and how do you manage boundaries?

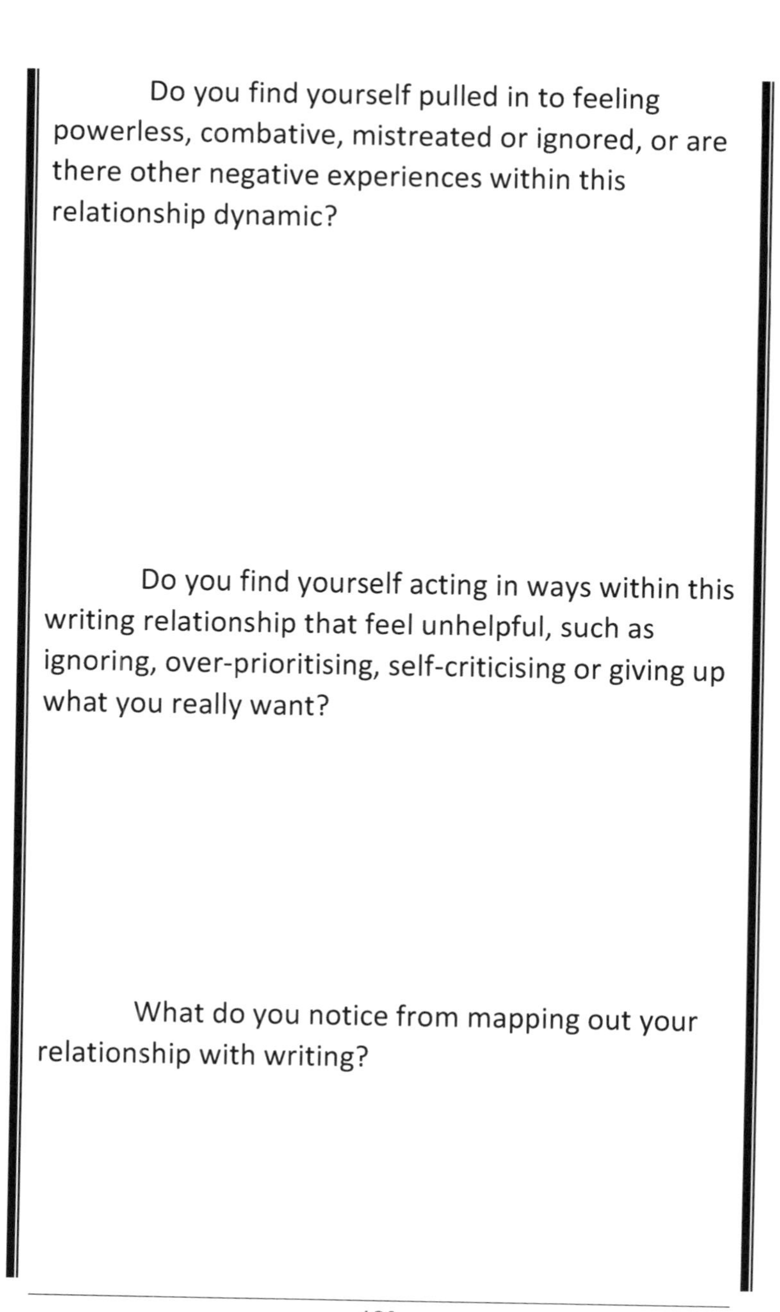

Do you find yourself pulled in to feeling powerless, combative, mistreated or ignored, or are there other negative experiences within this relationship dynamic?

Do you find yourself acting in ways within this writing relationship that feel unhelpful, such as ignoring, over-prioritising, self-criticising or giving up what you really want?

What do you notice from mapping out your relationship with writing?

Are these dynamics familiar to you from other relationships, past or present?

*Is there anything you'd like to do differently in the relationship with writing?

PLAYFULNESS

Children use play to make sense of their world, test out roles, practise skills and interaction, process their emotions, escape, connect and grow.[24] This is made possible by 'buying in' to the magic of play. A young child doesn't pick up a building block and say, 'Now I'll pretend this is a phone like the one you use, Mummy'; he says, 'Hello?'

Play in adults

Playfulness in adults is linked to spontaneity and creativity.[25] For some writing sessions, you can choose to take a playful approach to the process of writing. That is to say, not being tied to specific ways of working or expectation of a goal, as the process itself becomes the play. One element of play is experimentation. Children (and baby animals) try different strategies and roles to prepare themselves before committing to next steps in the real world. If drafting could be perceived as play, this might encourage creativity and reduce the restrictive impact of internal judgements.

Playful content and process

Playfulness in the content of writing could relate to many aspects, including form, voice, humour and red herrings. Unpredictability or the art of surprise can be loud and disorientating or quiet and subtle. It can be a character who isn't what you think, a story that bends into an unexpected shape, or outrageously different from the offset, forcing the reader into a magical world.

Playfulness in the process of writing can include using prompts, timers, co-writing, speed writing, deliberately changing form or content or taking part in generative writing workshops.

You could consider playful approaches to writing as an act of 'letting go', and this is likely to be more challenging to writers who prefer to maintain a strong sense of control.

*What does 'playfulness' mean to you in the context of HOW somebody writes?

*What could ‘playfulness’ mean in WHAT they write?

*Can you think of examples of playfulness in your own work?

What was your experience of it at the time you wrote a particular piece?

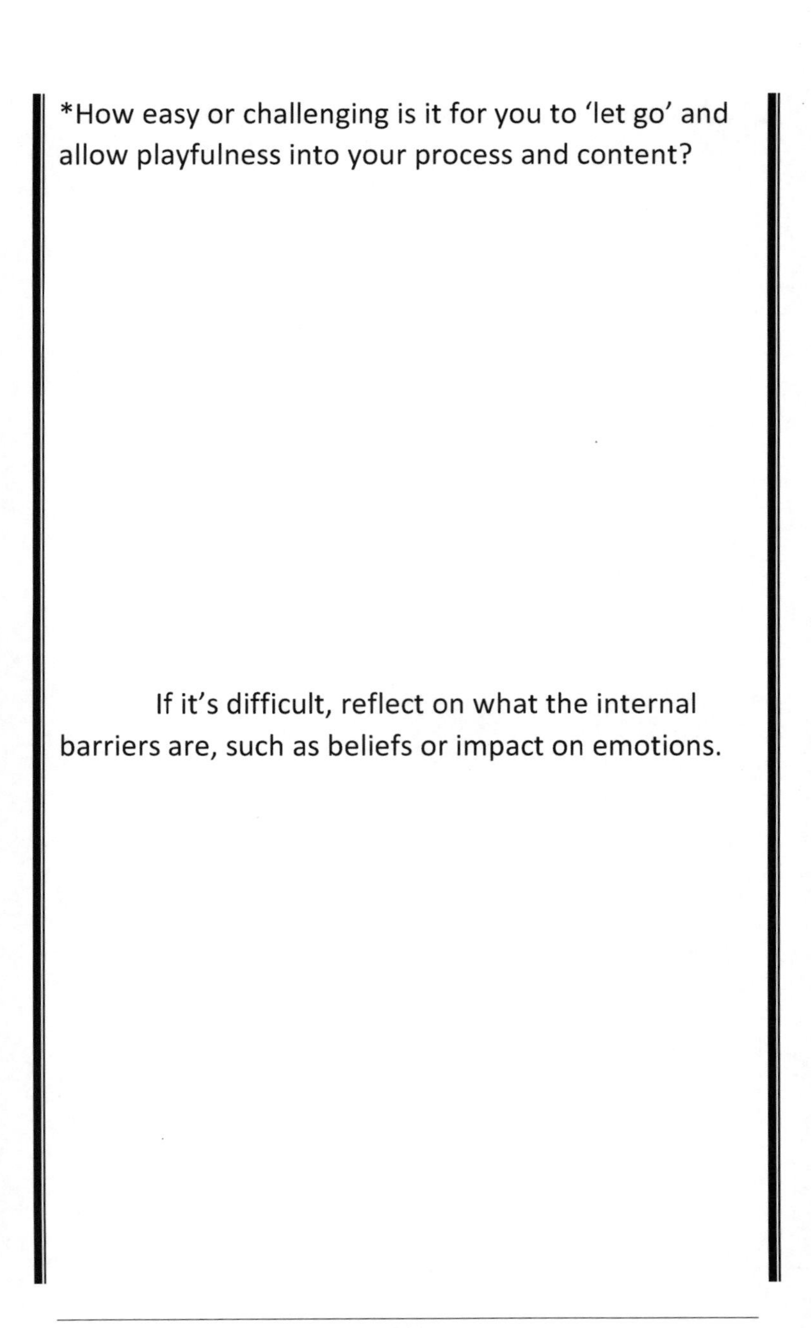

*How easy or challenging is it for you to 'let go' and allow playfulness into your process and content?

If it's difficult, reflect on what the internal barriers are, such as beliefs or impact on emotions.

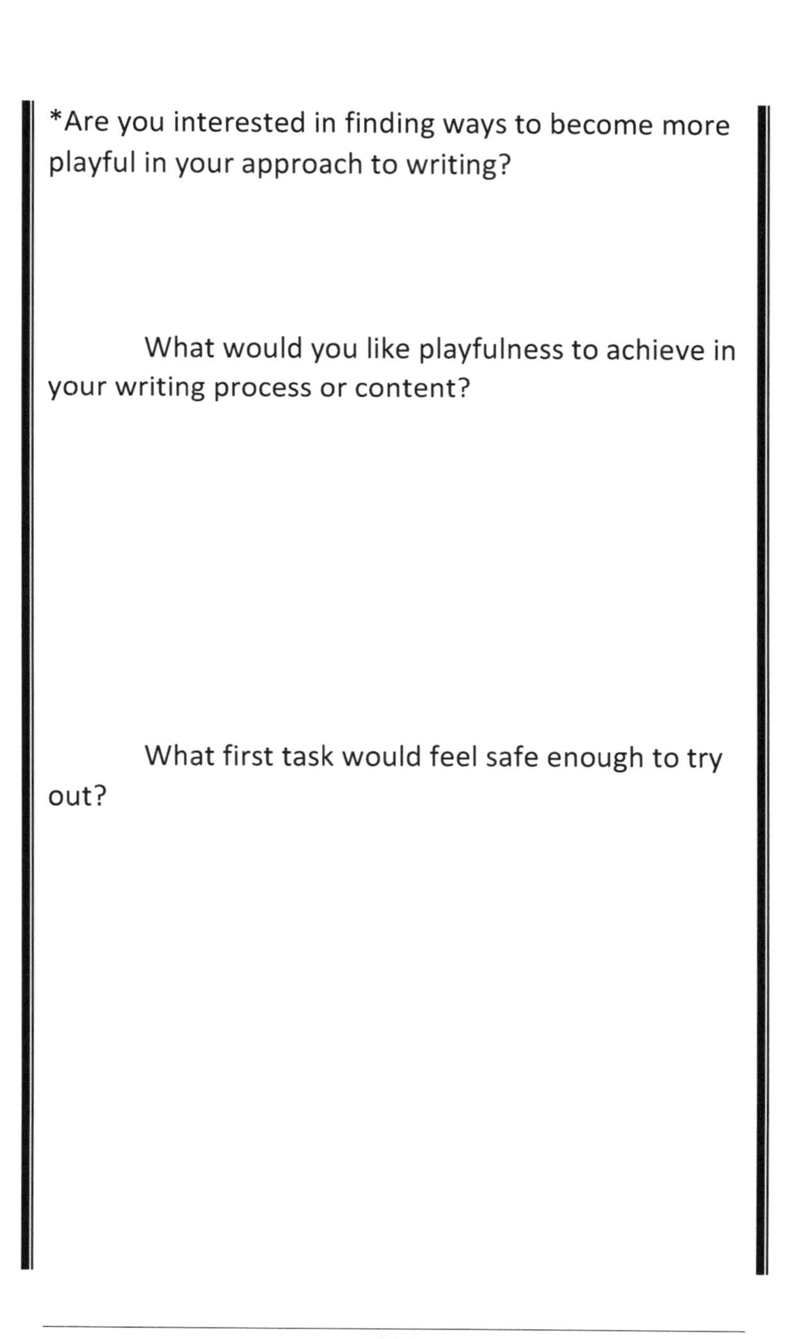

*Are you interested in finding ways to become more playful in your approach to writing?

What would you like playfulness to achieve in your writing process or content?

What first task would feel safe enough to try out?

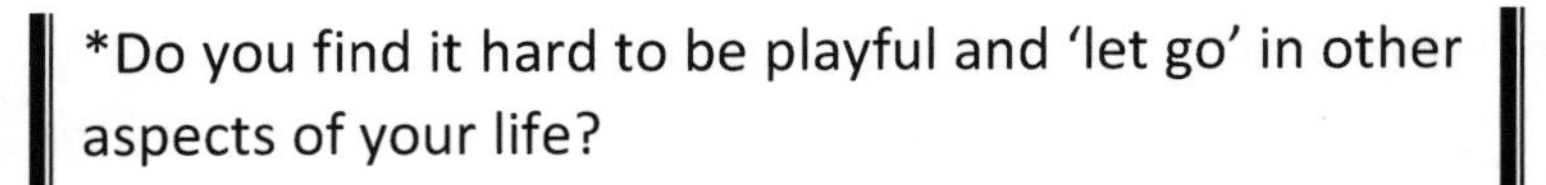

*Do you find it hard to be playful and 'let go' in other aspects of your life?

If so, can you pick out what 'rules' you might have inherited about playfulness in adults (e.g. it's disingenuous, only for kids, isn't serious work, risks being seen as incompetent or isn't safe)

You may want to consider where these rules or discomfort came from and how much you wish to hold onto these rules.

*Can you think of a time that you were playful in your adult life and it had a positive impact on you?

Immersing yourself in that memory might help reduce a sense of unease or fear of 'letting go' or increase the opportunity to let go in the future.

What small step could you take by yourself or with a trusted other to allow yourself an experience in which you can be playful?

Hide and Seek

Some types of writing, such as literary novels, poetry or flash fiction, may intend to use symbolism and subtlety to allow the reader to find meaning themselves rather than using explicit description. We could compare this to a game of hide and seek.

But you could also be playing this game with yourself. Your mind might have much to tell you through code, waiting for your readiness to reveal its layered meaning.

Emotions and longings can be hidden from our conscious awareness. However, they may reveal themselves in coded form, including through dreams.[26] Similarly, hidden elements of our mind sometimes reveal themselves through our prose and poetry, should we choose to pay attention.

Layers of meaning and symbolism

In the introduction to this book, it states:

In writing, as in dreams, there is both the manifest content (what the story appears to be about) and the latent content (symbolic meaning).

As with dream-work, stepping back from characters, plot and context can reveal longings and complex, contradictory feelings in a way that increases self-knowledge.[27]

The unconscious mind can communicate to the conscious mind –or let something slip – via the safety of symbols. Elements of our history, trauma, fears, disappointments and desires that our mind tries to prevent entering our awareness can transform into a palatable, less threatening form.

Freud used the technique of free association with his patients, in which symbols from dreams were taken and, prompted by that dream element, the patient said whatever came to mind. We can take a similar playful approach to our own work.

For example, if your repeated colour was red, you may list:

Danger, flag, hot, kiss, burn, running a temperature, bleed, scar tissue, the dress I wore for my thirtieth birthday, heart, angry, passionate, screaming, scalding, viper, stab, revenge.

Using the answers you gave in the chapter 'Repetition', you can explore what associations arise. You could do this by recording a voice note, drawing a spider diagram, creating a word association list or any other method that helps you chain and link.

Include words, images, memories and phrases. Go as fast as you can without trying to consider whether the answer is 'sensible' or not.

Colour:

Object:

Body part:

Word or sound:

Sensory detail:

You may find that the longer you go on with each prompt, the more abstract, or less obviously linked, the answers are. This could show that you are accessing more deeply buried connections.

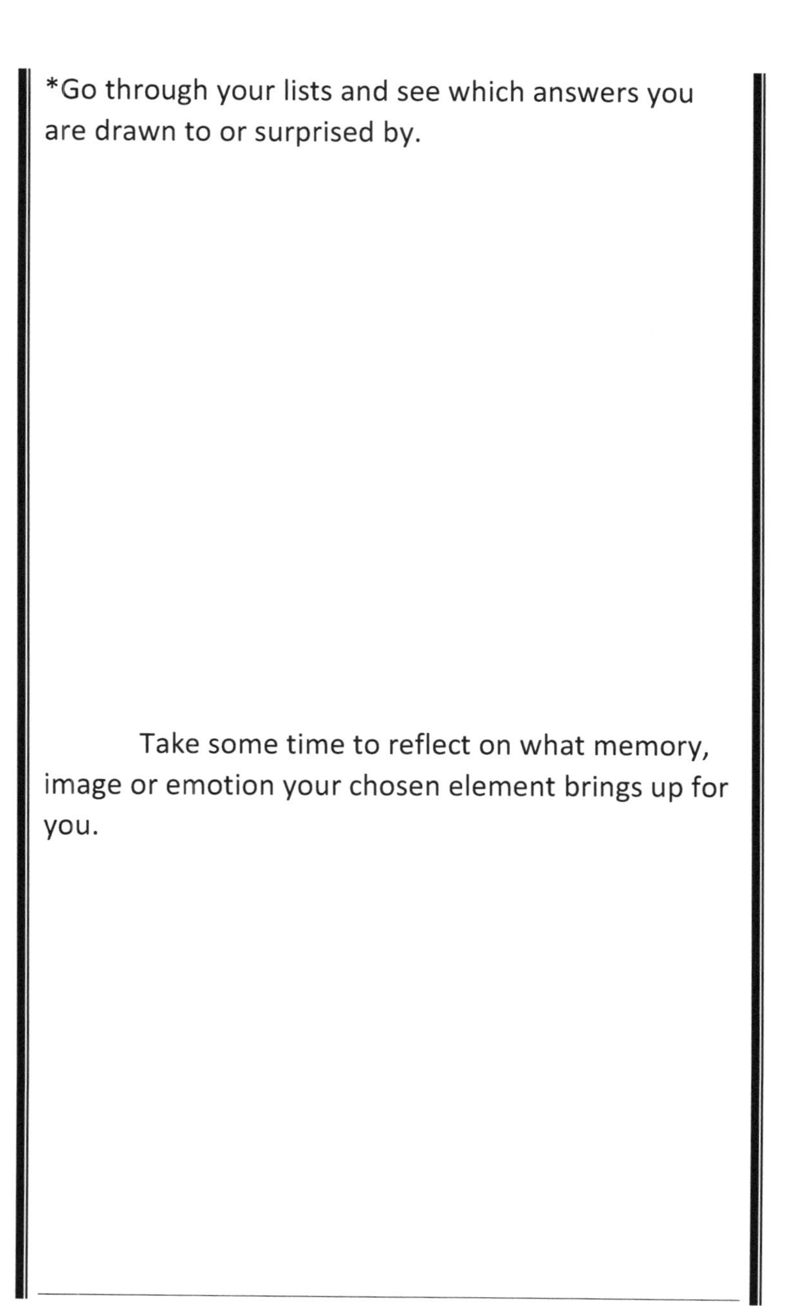

*Go through your lists and see which answers you are drawn to or surprised by.

Take some time to reflect on what memory, image or emotion your chosen element brings up for you.

Use the highlighted words as writing prompts, with 'permission' for your mind to explore further, as creatively as possible. You can choose to keep this fictionalised (which may help your defences stay lowered) or you might want to write a personally relevant piece of reflection or memoir as expressive writing.

What has emerged from your new piece of work? How might it add to an understanding of yourself?

THE WRITING SELF

Do I contradict myself?

Very well then I contradict myself,

(I am large, I contain multitudes.)[28]

Walt Whitman

*How would you describe your 'writer-self'?

*How does this compare to how you describe yourself in other areas of life?

What different states or parts of yourself do you bring to writing and which are not invited to the writing desk? You might find it illuminating to consider which ones play a more significant role when you write and what their impact is on both the process and content of your work. Your answers may differ according to the nature of the piece you are working on.

*Use the list below to consider which elements of yourself were present last time you wrote.

Focused

Self-assured

Playful

Vulnerable

Reflective

Brave

Energised

Emotional

Critical

Speedy

Precise

Challenged

*Make notes of the value each state could bring to specific tasks or types of writing, and which you wish to be more careful about. You can add your own categories.

*What have you noticed from doing this task?

What are the implications for you?

Function of Writing

When we have been asked *why* we write, we will have given various reasons. As complex creatures, we tend to have many aspects to our motivation, not just the one or two we are used to telling ourselves and others. You may be interested in scratching below the surface explanation to discover a broader range of motivations.

There are numerous reasons why we write. Even if a primary reason is to earn money (for those who do), then why *writing in particular*?

*Answering as quickly as you can, what are the top three reasons why you write?

By identifying the drivers behind why we write, we can use them as a guiding compass when we feel deflated, overwhelmed, doubting, disappointed or stuck in the writing life. Some of the reasons might show you how valuable your words are and that protecting your writing time is an important aspect of living an authentic life. Other reasons might indicate that writing is trying to fulfil a function that you could address via other ways that are not writing-related.

There are so many aspects to writing that they won't all be covered by this exercise. However, you may find it useful to start with the prompts here, then reflect on any other motivational factors that are salient to you.

*Were you ever TOLD that you should write or could be a writer? Or conversely, told that you were no good at writing, wouldn't make it or were given the message that it wasn't for someone like you?

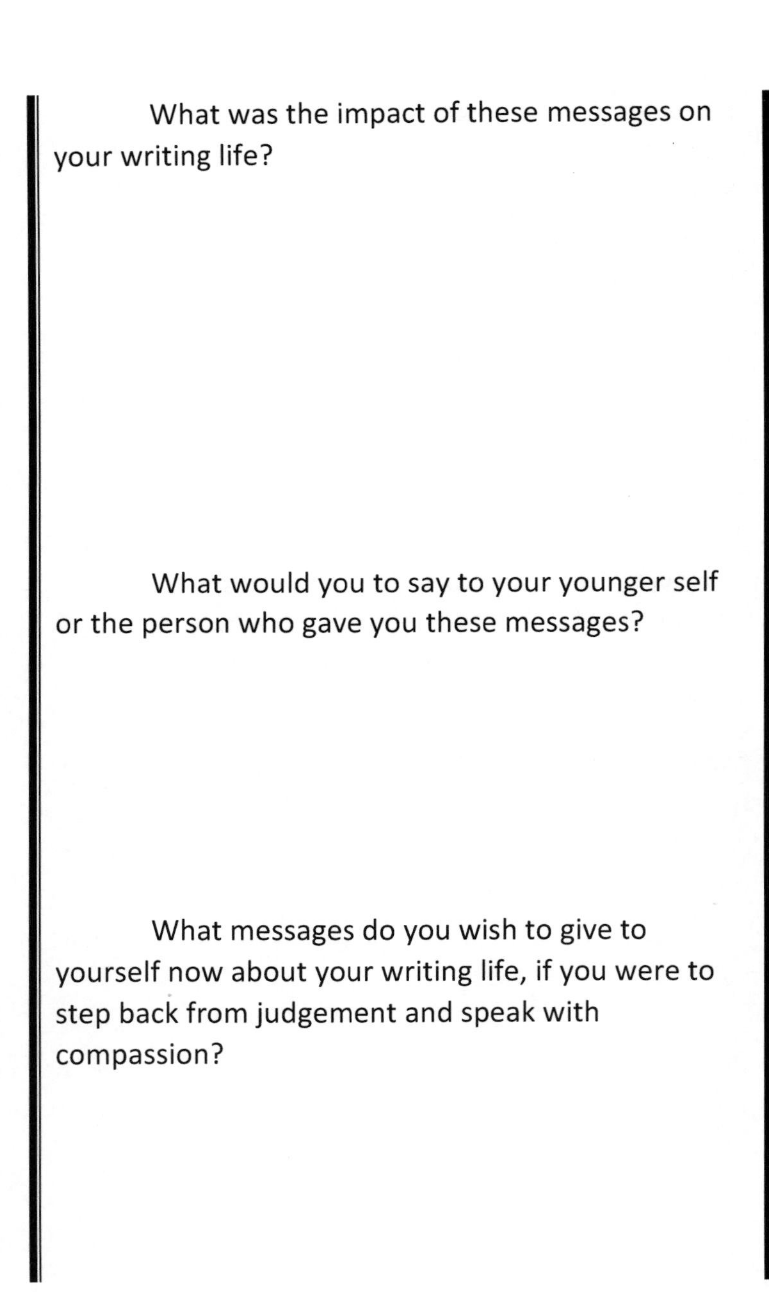

What was the impact of these messages on your writing life?

What would you to say to your younger self or the person who gave you these messages?

What messages do you wish to give to yourself now about your writing life, if you were to step back from judgement and speak with compassion?

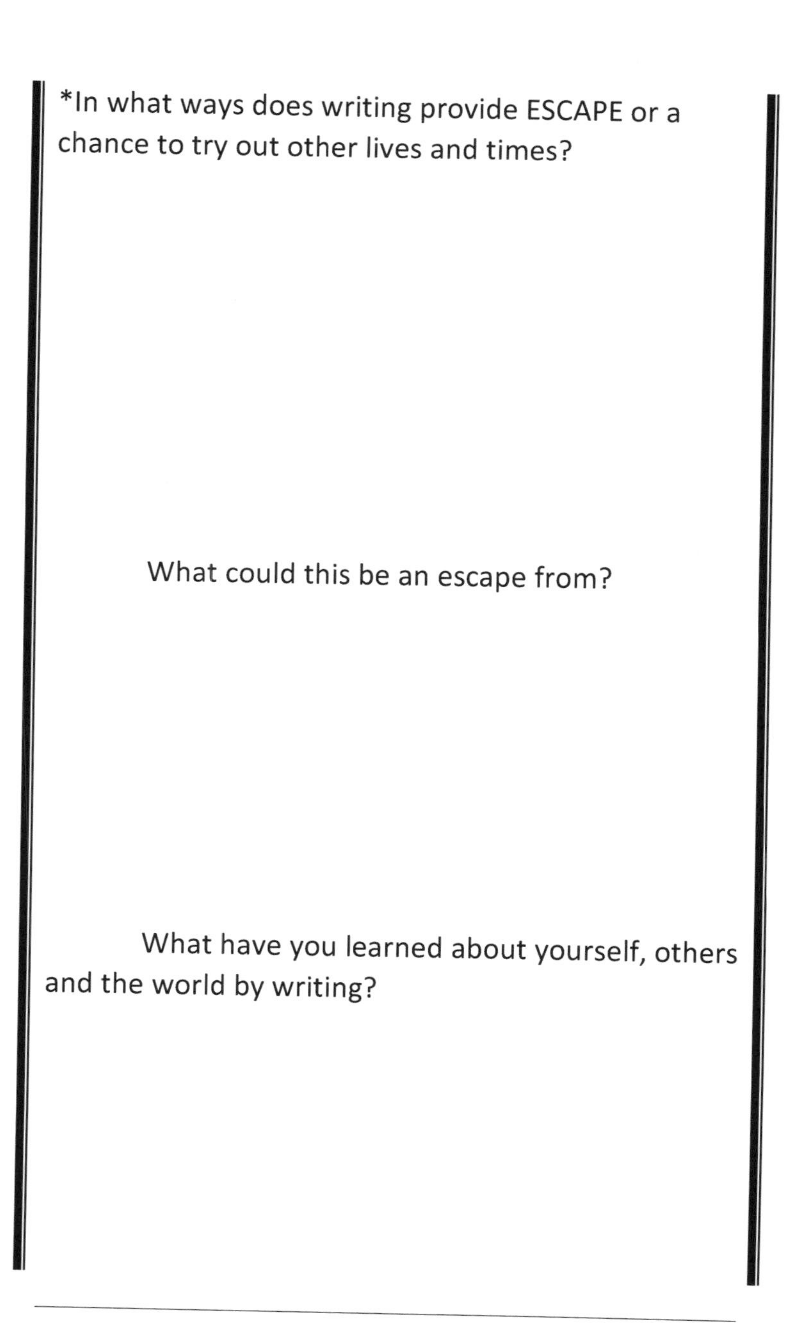

*In what ways does writing provide ESCAPE or a chance to try out other lives and times?

What could this be an escape from?

What have you learned about yourself, others and the world by writing?

How can you monitor when escape is helpful and the point at which this might tip into becoming unhelpful, for example as a way of avoiding dealing with real-world problems?

*Is writing a form of PLAY or EXPLORATION of other lives, times and possibilities?

In what ways does being playful or exploring in your writing impact on you?

Does writing give you some permission to play and explore that is not generally present in your everyday life?

What form did your play or exploration take in the past?

Do you wish for ways to increase opportunities for play and exploration in your life? What might this look like?

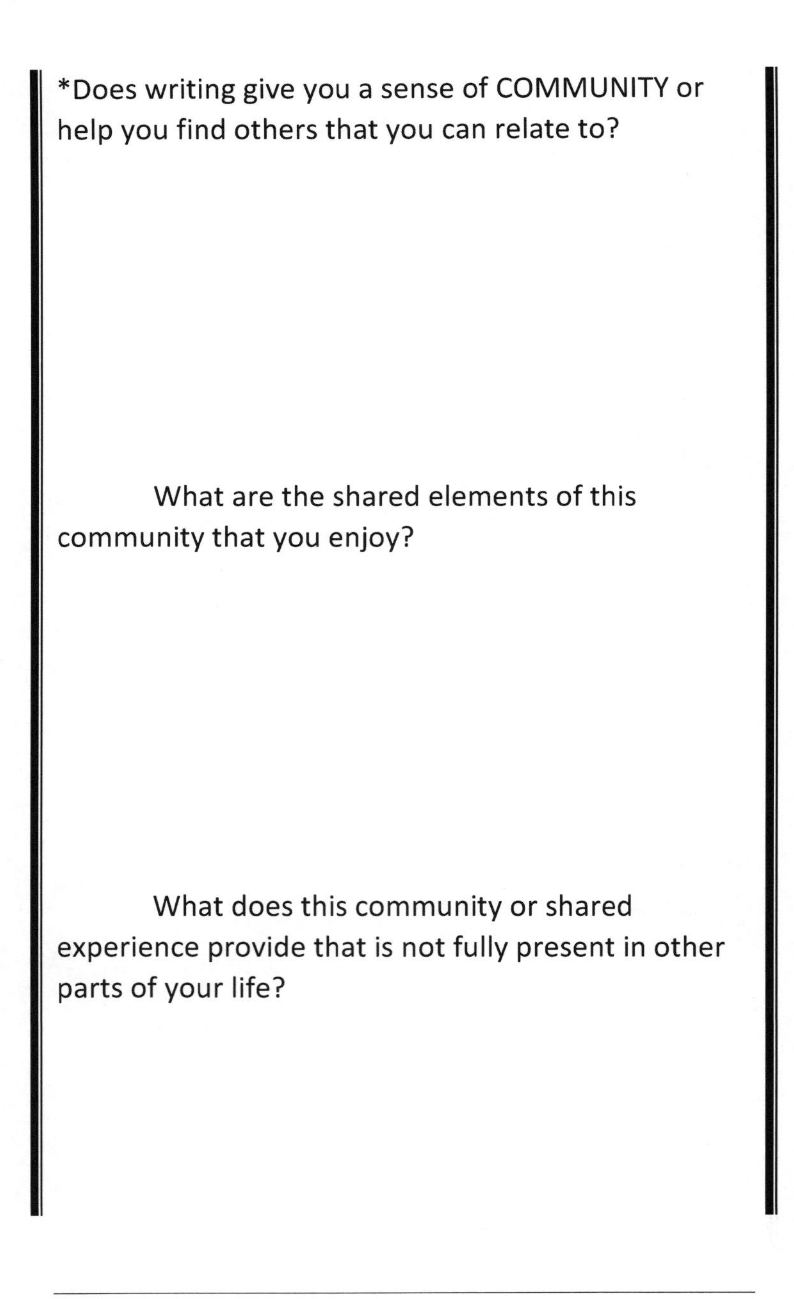

*Does writing give you a sense of COMMUNITY or help you find others that you can relate to?

What are the shared elements of this community that you enjoy?

What does this community or shared experience provide that is not fully present in other parts of your life?

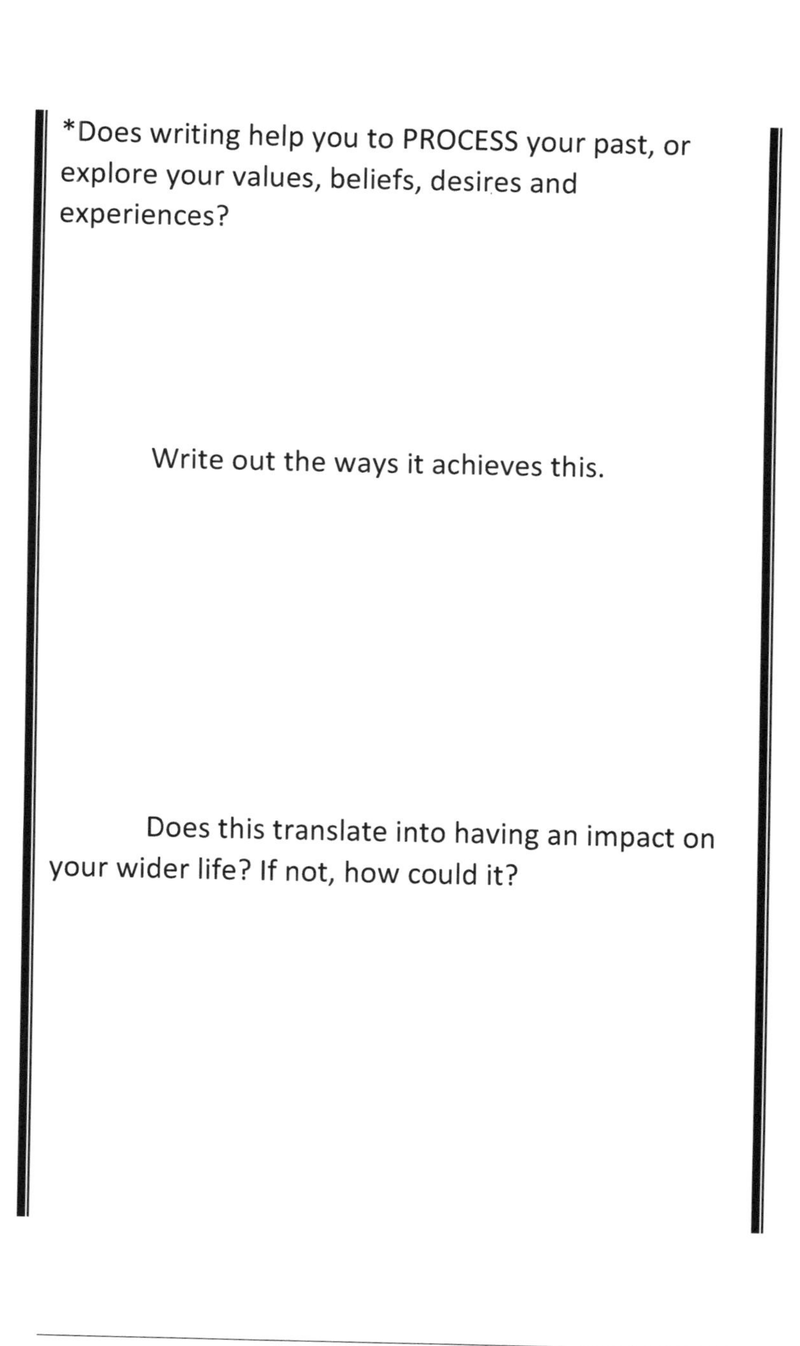

*Does writing help you to PROCESS your past, or explore your values, beliefs, desires and experiences?

Write out the ways it achieves this.

Does this translate into having an impact on your wider life? If not, how could it?

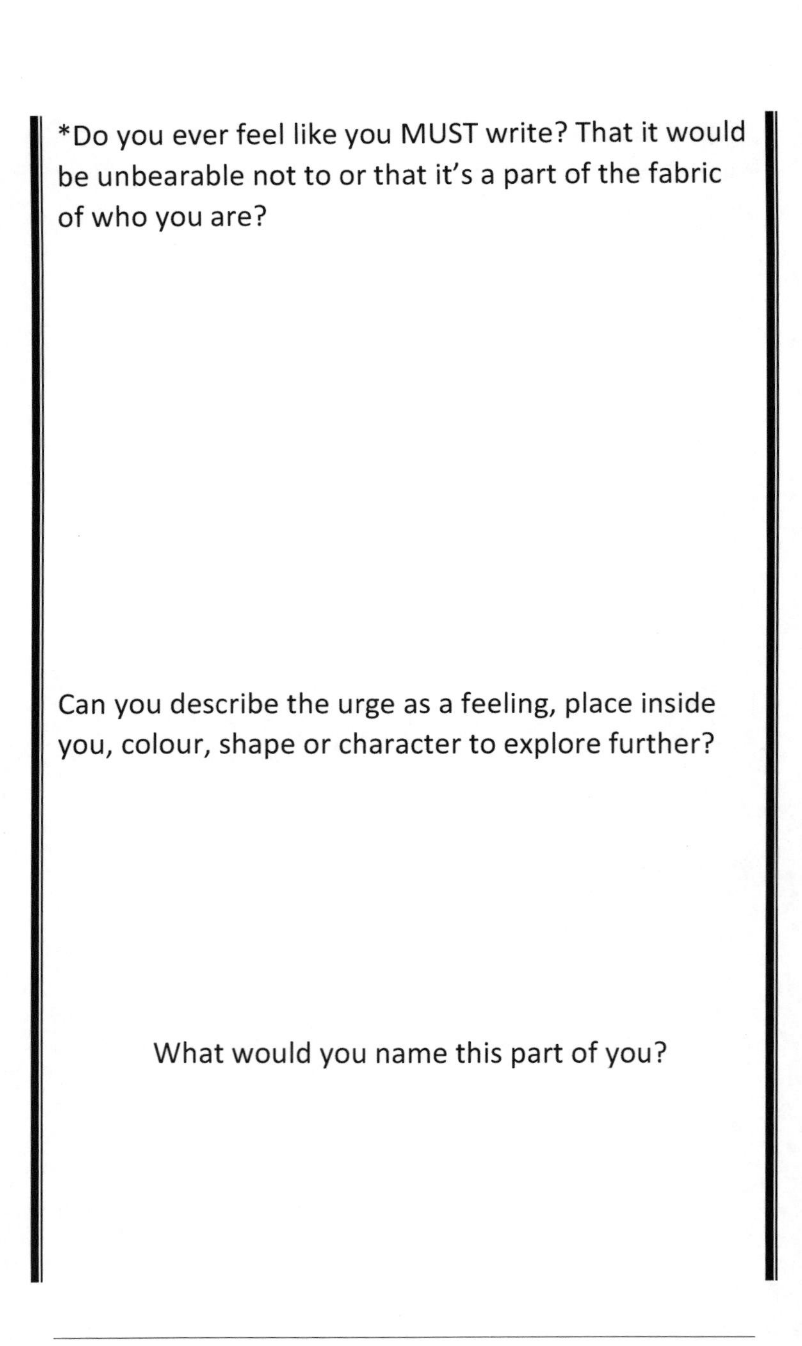

*Do you ever feel like you MUST write? That it would be unbearable not to or that it's a part of the fabric of who you are?

Can you describe the urge as a feeling, place inside you, colour, shape or character to explore further?

What would you name this part of you?

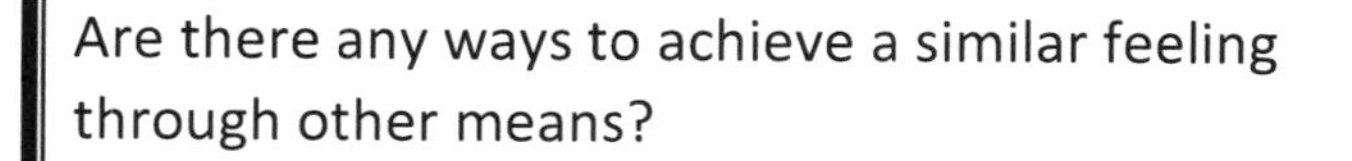

Are there any ways to achieve a similar feeling through other means?

Are there times when the 'MUST' actually starts to be unhelpful, and becomes a pressure? Or times when you don't allow yourself the joy or release of writing, despite this urge?

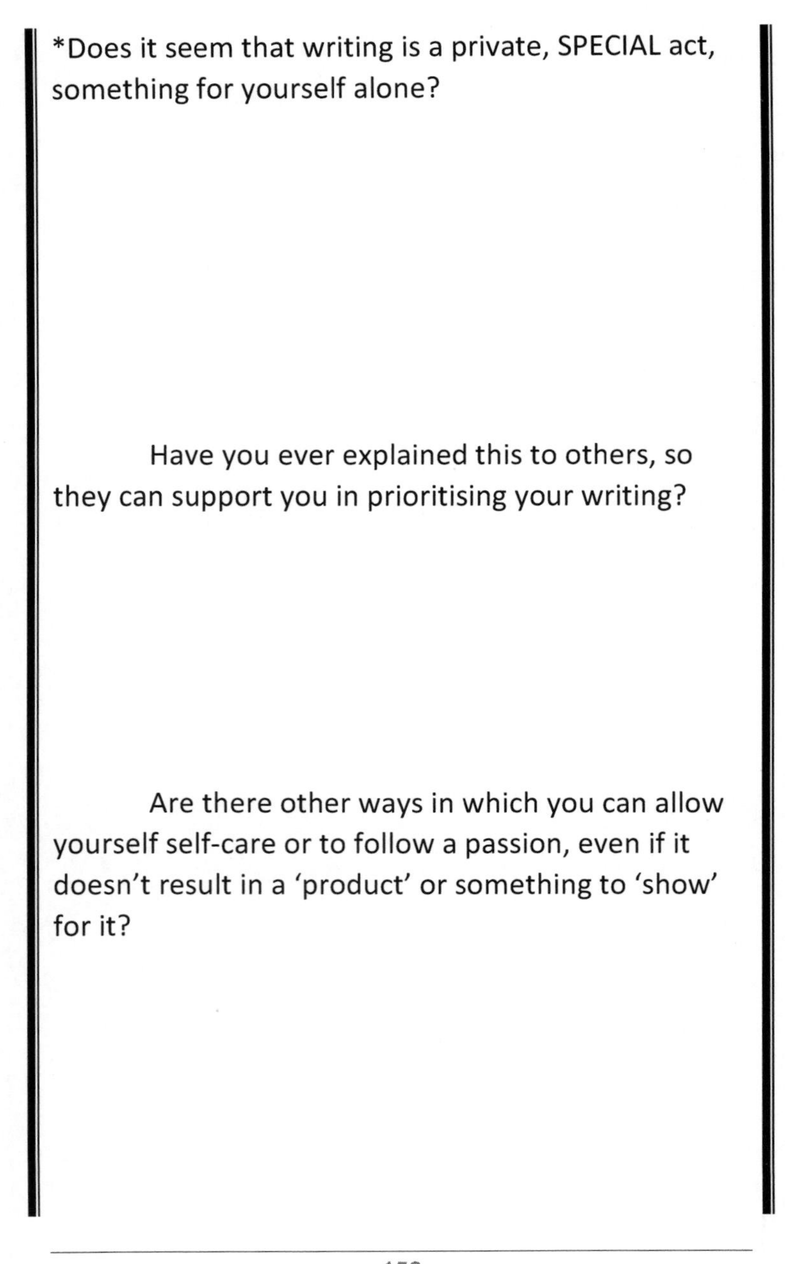

*Does it seem that writing is a private, SPECIAL act, something for yourself alone?

Have you ever explained this to others, so they can support you in prioritising your writing?

Are there other ways in which you can allow yourself self-care or to follow a passion, even if it doesn't result in a 'product' or something to 'show' for it?

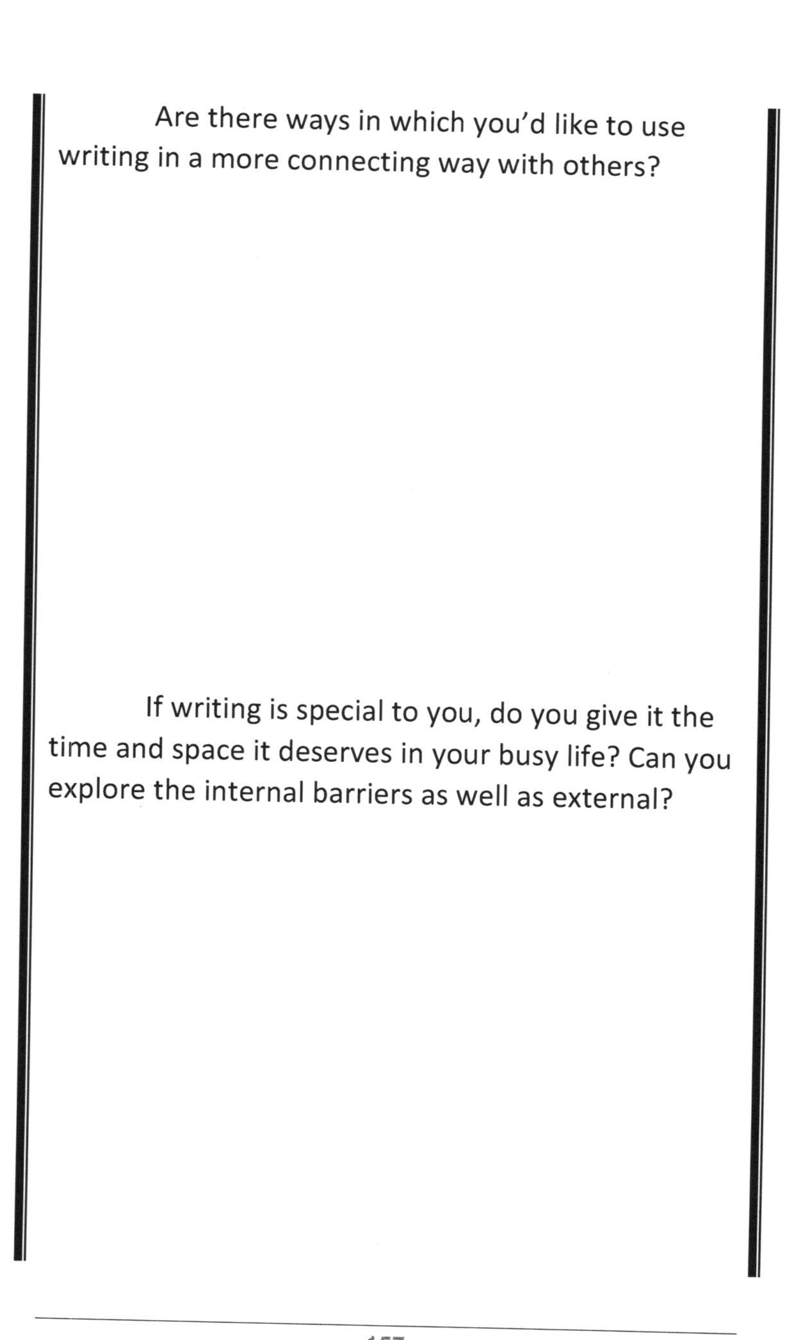

Are there ways in which you'd like to use writing in a more connecting way with others?

If writing is special to you, do you give it the time and space it deserves in your busy life? Can you explore the internal barriers as well as external?

*Do you write for the JOY of it, the pleasure of creating, a focus on language, an immersion in your creative world?

How would you describe your body, mind and behaviour when you most enjoy your writing?

If you write and find it does not bring pleasure, what is the impact of this on your thoughts, mood and writing behaviour? What would help you get through these periods?

How can you pay more attention to the positive aspects of your writing in the future, such as the impact on your wellbeing? Are there ways in which those joyful moments can help counterbalance the harsher side of your writing (and daily) life?

*Does writing provide an opportunity to COMMUNICATE and BE HEARD?

How meaningful to you is it to have a voice and be heard?

Is this something that has been hard to achieve in the past through more direct means?

Review your current or planned next piece of writing. Will it achieve your aim of communicating and being heard?

Think about other ways you can try to communicate and be heard that are not related to writing. What could you take from your writing skills to help with this?

Following this task, you may find it useful to articulate or map out all the reasons you write, watching out for how they intersect. Take some time to notice the value of your writing life and writer-self.

There may be some functions that you hope writing will achieve, yet it never seems to quite hit the mark. Or the initial 'hit' doesn't last long, leaving you feeling hopeless or in need of pushing yourself again to try to meet your version of 'success'. Examples of what you may consciously or unconsciously hope to gain from writing include feeling 'good enough' or leaving your mark on the world.

*Do any of these apply to you? If so, does writing actually achieve this goal, and how long does that feeling of achievement last for?

- To feel good enough

- To prove yourself

- To feel like you fit in

- To be more like someone you admire

- To be better understood

- To feel less isolated

- To get some recognition

- To feel like you've 'made it'

- To reduce uncertainty

- To feel productive enough

- To leave your mark on the world

If you find that, for you, writing doesn’t meet a goal, perhaps this particular element is one that is not (entirely) solvable via writing. In effect, you may be trying to fill a bucket that has a hole in; the sand you spade in makes it appear that the bucket is filling up, but at the same time, sand is escaping from the bottom, making it a task that is doomed to fail or one that needs continuous effort.

*Take some time to step back and notice any ways in which writing is NOT achieving what you fantasise it will. Review the multiple reasons behind why you write and examine the other ways in which it is valuable to you.

*If there are particular ‘holes in your bucket’ (such as not feeling good enough), what could be a helpful, realistic first step to acknowledging or addressing this outside of writing?

Reflections

It is a gift to yourself and your writing to take the time to reflect.

Your writing matters.

You matter.

Reviewing your answers in the future or revisiting certain topics that are pertinent to you could provide one way of maintaining your reflective processes and noticing change over time.

*What are the main points you wish to recall from using this workbook?

*What would you like to return to in the future?

*What actions are you committing yourself to take?

[1] Carty (2019). Hall of mirrors: Aspects of the writer self. *Ellipsis Zine*.
[2] Freud (1900). *Interpretation of Dreams*.
[3] Hutton-Carty (2018). Writing and the unconscious. *Fiction Southeast*.
[4] Tierney & Farmer (2002). Creative self-efficacy: its potential antecedents and relationship to creative performance. *Academy of Management Journal*.
[5] Bandura & Lock (2003). Negative self-efficacy and goal effects revisited. *Journal of Applied Psychology*.
[6] Bandura (2011). On the functional properties of perceived self-efficacy revisited. *Journal of Management*.
[7] Beck (1976). *Cognitive Therapy and the Emotional Disorders*.
[8] Søren Kierkegaard, *The Concept of Anxiety: A Simple Psychologically Orienting Deliberation on the Dogmatic Issue of Hereditary Sin*.
[9] Tottenham & Sheridan (2010). A review of adversity, the amygdala and the hippocampus: a consideration of developmental timing. *Frontiers in Human Neuroscience*.
[10] Goldstein & Naglieri (2014). *Handbook of Executive Functioning*.
[11] Zelazo & Carlson (2020). The neurodevelopment of executive function skills. *Psychology & Neuroscience*.
[12] Doyle (1998). The writer tells: the creative process in the writing of literary fiction. *Creative Research Journal.*
[13] Doyle (2017). Creative flow as a unique cognitive process. *Frontiers in Psychology.*
[14] Pagon (2002). Why does bright light cause some people to sneeze?. *Scientific American*.
[15] Csikszentmihalyi (1986) cited in Goleman H. (1996) *Emotional Intelligence*.
[16] Csikszentmihalyi (1990). *Flow: The psychology of optimal experience.*

[17] Webster et al., *Playfulness: Development of a Measure with Workplace Implications.*
[18] Csikszentmihalyi & LeFevre (1989). Optimal experience in work and leisure. *Journal of Personality and Social Psychology.*
[19] Britton et al. (2010). Development of anxiety: the role of threat appraisal and fear learning. *Depression & Anxiety.*
[20] Frost et al. (1990) The dimensions of perfectionism. *Cognitive Therapy and Research.*
[21] Hewitt & Flett (2004). Multidimensional Perfectionism Scale (MPS).
[22] Pennebaker & Smyth. (2016). *Opening Up by Writing Down.*
[23] Freud (1914). *Remembering, Repeating and Working-Through.*
[24] Whitebread et al. (2017). The role of play in children's development: a review of the evidence (research summary). The LEGO Foundation.
[25] Glynn & Webster (1992). The Adult Playfulness Scale: An initial assessment. *Psychological Reports.*
[26] Freud (1900). *The Interpretation of Dreams.*
[27] Hutton-Carty (2018). Writing and the unconscious. *Fiction Southeast.*
[28] Whitman (1855). *Leaves of Grass.*

Printed in Poland
by Amazon Fulfillment
Poland Sp. z o.o., Wrocław